CLASSIFICATION: POETRY

A CIP catalogue record for this book is available from the British Library.

Printed and bound in Great Britain.

Paper used in the production of books published by United Press comes only from sustainable forests.

ISBN 978-0-85781-018-2

First published in Great Britain in 2011 by
United Press Ltd
Admail 3735
London
EC1B 1JB
Tel: 0844 800 9177
Fax: 0844 800 9178
All Rights Reserved

www.unitedpress.co.uk

Maltman, Orpington, Enid Rosemary Daley, Islington, Rosalind Berwald, Stanmore, Henry James Wood, Westcliff-on-Sea, Charmaine Fletcher, Basildon.

SOUTH WEST AND CHANNEL ISLANDS - Pages 60-81

Lynn Parr, Looe, Jeanne Bradley, Torquay, Indranee de Silva, Frome, Gillian Minter, Chippenham, Sofy Bevan, Gloucester, Frances Lowe, Bridgwater, Mark Wynne, Westbury, Lesley Bairstow, Marlborough, Judith Marr, Weston-super-Mare, Joan Knight, Portishead, Marnie Ellis, Wells, Joy Edwards, Bradninch, R T J Harris, Tiverton, John Rustage, Winchcombe, Audrey Dowsett, Lechdale, Katie Grant, Dorchester, Pamela Davies, Bournemouth, Dawn Cawley, Plymouth, Talitha Black, Bideford, Richard Thomas, Totnes, Jo Heydon, Rock, Elvena Grace, Sweetshouse, Carl Michael Dowden, St Martin, Margaret Boden-Heaume, Guernsey, Anne Ashman, St Ann's Chapel, Trisha Driscoll, Polzeath, Susan Coles, Bath.

EAST ANGLIA - Pages 83-91

John Harris, Heacham, Derek Lane, Peterborough, Nancy Stephenson, Cambridge, Leila Anani, Stowmarket, Kate Buck, Diss, John Cates, Cambridge, Lenore Abraham, Cambridge, Nicholas Hills, King's Lynn, Doreen Hale, Sheringham, Greta Robinson, Ipswich, Marilyn Lyne, Hadleigh.

EAST MIDLANDS - Pages 93-108

Janice Taylor, Ripley, Gillian Hartley, Repton, Mo Ward, Hinckley, Eileen Wale, Selston, Natalie Beck, Heanor, Trudi Macagnino, Southwell, Jackie Heald, Wellingborough, Richard Savage, Long Eaton, Lauren Hall, Sudbrooke, Hugh Rogers, Scunthorpe, Keith Linley, Lincoln, Tina Negus, Grantham, Charlotte Hoare, Lincoln, Alison Fairchild, Horncastle, Heather Chandler, Ashby-de-la-Zouch, Ena Swain, Loughborough, Richard Hulett, Kettering, Carol Tilley, Ilkeston, Rodney Ward, Chesterfield, James Hawkins Woodward, Lullington, Alan Robinson, Warnall, Monica Norgate, Oakham.

WEST MIDLANDS - Pages 110-129

Lorna Meehan, Oldbury, Sylvia Lees, Rugeley, Bethan Ford-Williams, Walsall, Louise Henly, Wolverhampton, David Grayling, Leamington Spa, Victoria Maguire, Sutton Coldfield, Penelope Hewitt, Birmingham, Patrick Derwent, Kenilworth, Rosy Reilly, Bedworth, William Joss, Whatcote, Laura Smith, Bulkington, J R Heron, Newcastle-under-Lyme, Dave Brough, Southam, Tracy Davidson, Stratford-upon-Avon, Philip Williams, Cheslyn Hay, Cindy Faulkner, Cannock, Simon H Lindley, Cheadle, Ian Ward, Wasall, Jim Davies, Church Stretton, Alexander Ward, Stafford, Ian Michael Duncan, Oswestry, Alison Perry, Cleeve Prior, Jean M Hill, Stoke-on-Trent, Chloe Bridget Trumper, Newport, Pam Gosling, Redditch, Elizabeth Marshall, Wombourne, Dorothy Headland, Shrewsbury, Louise Pell, Goodrich, Hollie Lewis, St Weonards.

NORTH WEST - Pages 131-149

Esther Sterry, Neston, Jean Riggini, Manchester, Frances Heyes, St Helens, Penny Kimber, Lymm, Lauren Cooper, Burnley, Lynn Noone, Swinton, Will Ekbery, Wallasey, Sylvia Wilkinson, Bury, Rachel Cole, Astley Village, Lucy Perry, Lancaster, Marjory Houlihan, Bolton, Liz Kavanagh, Liverpool, June Brooks, Upholland, John Harrison, Hutton, Jean Watson, Crosby, John Reynolds, Prenton, Muriel Miller, Blackburn, Elizabeth Ware, Penrith, Dennis Toye, Darlton-in-Furness, Darren Kelly, Southport, Matthew Birchall, Ashton-in-Makerfield, Rachael Knott, Congleton, Lee Hughes, Ellesmere Port, Margaret Harris, Chester.

NORTH EAST - Pages 151-171

Fenella Berry, Halifax, Sandra Wiggins, Leeds, Mary Loy, Bradford, Margaret Squire, Elland, Patrick Mennell, Hull, Clare Lupino, Hebden Bridge, Anna Lawson, Baildon, Audrey McIlvain, Scarborough, Robert Morley, Doncaster, Jerry Dowson, Houghton-le-Spring, Lynn Widdows, Harrogate, Duane Boyd, Ripon, Angela Dinan, Driffield, Anne Broadbent, Honley

Holmfirth, Gavin Extence, Sheffield, Philip Cranswick, Rotherham, Derek Greenacre, Morpeth, Marjorie Lacy, South Elmsall, David Thomson, Newcastle-upon-Tyne, Rob Turnbull, Haltwhistle, Kathleen J Jinks, Middlesbrough, Elaine D Scullion, Dunston, Mary Atkinson, Alnwick, Jennifer Gordon-Russell, Morpeth, Betty Hewitt, Darlington, Jack Howard, Crook, George Carrick, Cramlington, Irene Anderson, Leadgate.

NORTHERN IRELAND - Pages 173-175

Hubert Boyle, Magherafelt, Niamh O'Kane, Limavady, Rosie Hogan-Diamond, Ballymena, James Wilson, Ballyclare.

WALES - Pages 177-189

Amy Angharad Jones, Cowbridge, Karla Brading, Merthyr Tydfil, David Cirell, Barry, Simon Hicks, Chepstow, Janet Williams, Newport, Joanne Newton, Cemmaes, Jean Ruston, Talybunt-on-Usk, Vera Phillips, Newport, Lindsay Hurlow, Swansea, Peter Hughes, Anglesey, Janet Hughes, Montgomery, Richard Lloyd, Newcastle Emlyn, James Hayward, Bargoed, Lianne Jones, Cardiff.

SCOTLAND - Pages 191-207

N J Bain, Duns, Gabriel Dennis, Blairgowrie, Julie Martis, Hamilton, Thomas Craig, Hamilton, J Elliott, Ayr, Carole Bone, Glasgow, Patricia Turner, Dalbeattie, Josephine Sumner, Tain, Muriel Ferrier, Dundee, Brian Sutherland, Prestonpans, Maggi Macleod, Caithness, Teresa Doughty, Fife, Jacqueline Bain, Paisley, Valerie MacGregor, Edinburgh, Linda Mackie, Saltcoats, Jane Ritchie, Dundonald, Laura Bennison, Whitecairns, Rona Harvey, Brodie, Myra Wimpenny, Kirkcaldy, Chris Cameron, Kelso, John McGowan, Annan.

South East

TRANSPORTS OF DELIGHT

I guess that you, like I, delight
That these tiny vessels
Can carry such rich and wondrous cargoes,
Plying the several seas
Of fact and imagination.

Dock me always, therefore
Among books,
These transports of delight,
That make us travellers through time and space
With fine minds for companions.

And let us all delight
To see the mighty fear them,
Bar and burn them, scar and spurn them;
They're not so insubstantial,
For whatever else it seems
These flimsy, inky scratchings
Are the nets that catch our dreams.

Alan Robertson, Caddington, Bedfordshire

THE DRESS

I saw it! So gorgeous! Hanging on a rail
I knew, I had to have it, hoped it was for sale
I felt it, I sized it, hoped it would not fail
I tried it, it fitted. And now I could not wail
I bought it, I wore it, pulled a handsome male.
I touched it, I smoothed it, wore it with a veil,
I hung it, all perfect, now it told a tale,
I see it, so gorgeous, hanging on *my* rail!

Karen Shevlane, Shefford, Bedfordshire

SUMMER MORNING

Remember Miranda
Summer mornings long ago
When you would rise before the world awakened
And wander in the early hours' sunshine
You loved to stroll barefoot
On the dew moist short grass
And enjoy the bright border flowers
The deep blue cornflowers and gaudy red poppies
You would sing softly
Now wanting to spoil the birdsong
For this was your own world
I would watch you from the open window
Your long cotton dress moving gently in the breeze
But now you move slowly and stiffly, and need a cane
Remember, Miranda, remember,
Those summer morns so long ago
When we were young
And the future day held so much promise.

Sean Gage, Ryde, Isle of Wight

WAITING AT THE PAINT SHOP

Waiting at the paint shop,
Rain puckered the car windscreen.
As we watched black notes roll and slop,
Wipers smeared across emulsion,

What's that music? asked my daughter.
It's Schubert's Winter Reise;
A lost smile; a lover's name carved
With a sharp stone in a frozen river.

Do you like it too?
Customers scuttled out clutching paint.
The song of lost loved glossed
Misty windows in arpeggios.

Tins of white bought for dusty walls,
Footprints left on sanded floors,
Deer prints brushed across a field, a solitary crow.
The singer's hair turning white in falling snow.

David Jones, Southampton, Hampshire

THESE DRY WOODEN BLOCKS

White, bitten to the quick, raw.
Here, a scab, picked until it puckered, angry.
Tiny beads glitter there across the palm, and a
Bump, calloused and dull from setting down
In words, things better said.

These dry wooden blocks are old.
Young enough to tremble as they make the tentative
Reach for a lover's breast.

They shake in the cold empty air.

Thomas Leather, Bracknell, Berkshire

PREJUDICE

The line is thrown
The die is cast
Will you submit and do what's asked?
The choice is yours to call it quits or
Remain encased in prejudice.

Let go and know, the horse is shod
The carriage awaits, the will of God.
Climb aboard and take the journey
To your core
Which once was left on distant shores.

Reclaim the self that has been split
Let the light now be lit
Its glow transcends hatred's darkest night
Together we can reclaim
Love's truest flight.

Karen Palmer, Aylesbury, Buckinghamshire

EASTER MORNING

No more for me the euphoria of other Easters.
When, swept along by waves of popular belief
I would exchange a warm and comfortable bed
For a windswept hill
To welcome in a dawn
Supposed to lift my spirit
Free my soul from ill.

While all around me waited
With upturned face towards the sky,
I closed my eyes in disbelief
Wondering what brought me here
And why I did not experience
Their joy and wonder
On this resurrection morn.

When the first light of dawn broke
With one accord they would lift
Their eyes towards the sun
To welcome in an Easter morning.
I could only bow my head
In lasting mourning.

Theodore Armstrong, Bedford, Bedfordshire

CHANGING COLOURS

The white silk scarf you gave me
the polished silver locket, honeymoon
photos in the summer sun gradually
changed their colour,
the hall door I varnished
the IKEA furniture assembled
before our first baby,
has now deepened in colour
and our marriage springs to mind
not lightened or deepened
but like the artist's palette
layers of colour upon colour.

Helena Boland, Barnet, Hertforshire

OCTOBER

Beautiful rain
Bouncing off concrete slabs
Scattering autumn leaves
And unsuspecting creatures

The dark demonic sky
Rushes past
Unloading its enemy
Onto a beautiful garden

Pummel and pound
Weep and soak
Break and divide
The ground, the seed,
The warm world

Faith Joanne, Basingstoke, Hampshire

I WOULD NOT DIE

I would not die for wanting you,
Though unrequited my love bloom
Nor rest at ease romance to please
And bless the graveness of the tomb.

I would still swoon through sunlit days
And moonlit pleasures this life holds,
E'en should your face no longer grace
My soliditude with sweet repose.

The world would still not cease to twirl
Nor stars deny to guide my fate
Should you but turn my love to spurn
My soul would not consume with hate.

Yet something in the day's sweet bliss
Which senses cannot understand
Would surely slip beyond my reach,
Were you not there to hold my hand.

And though this path be scarce the same,
I know that should you cease to care
The days would never dawn so bright
Nor any nights to these compare.

Emmie Bidston, Finchampstead, Berkshire

HEADING HOME

Something rushed you in the darkness
on the lane, late to the village.

It was your footsteps storming
mistward ahead,
clicking on mud-slicked stone.

You pitched to reach them,
never knowing
all this falling was
landing on your feet.

Adam Flint, Abingdon, Oxfordshire

AN ODE TO TECHNO

Travel down a frenetic tubule,
A tunnel of shaded fluorescence,
Irregular shapes cracked into the walls,
Frantic energy pushing behind,
Waters of crystalline luminosity,
A stretched incandescence of song,
Heights squirm vertically,
A wobbling, waffling, distorted wind,
Wafts stiflingly around,
Pulling into a rainbow-like kaleidoscope,
Whirring of whispered scrapes,
Vibrant echoes and reverberating green glare,
Resonant flutters rise high,
Drawback, attack again,
Lapse into extremities,
Fade in a bleeping of particles.

Julian Webb, Romsey, Hampshire

THE WIND DID HOWL

The wind did howl,
The rain did pour,
The trees did shake and creak.
The water came inside my door,
My roof had sprung a leak.

My feet were cold,
My socks were wet,
The bucket was no use.
It didn't look like stopping yet,
I wished I was a goose.

The lightning flashed,
The thunder rolled,
A tree fell through my ceiling.
The hole it left let in the cold,
I had a sinking feeling.

My barge went down,
I swam ashore,
The local pub awaited.
I now know things not known before,
Canals are overrated.

Edward Harris, Milton Keynes, Buckinghamshire

THE CHIMES OF ST MARY'S

I remember a home that once was,
Where many years passed and with them my youth,
Where my thoughts will fall into nostalgia,
The heart will sigh with memory's truth.

I can still hear the bells accompany me,
Over fields and hills onto her grounds,
Where I would sit alone and read a verse,
And dream of love to St Mary's sounds.

To her divine peal away I would fancy,
And wonder on what the morrow would bring.
Walk with the evening through her tranquil gardens,
Certain of naught but her hallowed ring.

And on a bench among the scattered stones,
Engraved with remembrances and soiled with time,
I think of those that lie here before me,
In eternal joy with St Mary's chime.

Now the seasons are turning, years ever passing,
And far from that home, far from her skies.
And though wishing more questing, desiring more roving,
I find myself missing sweet St Mary's cries.

Michael Rivers, Hemel Hempstead, Hertfordshire

THE LILAC FLOWER

The strong scented lilac sways gently in the night,
When people are in their homes, sleeping tight.

Its smooth-to-touch petals are softer than silk,
They rise out of their stems like teardrops of pink milk.

When the bud opens and out bursts a flower,
It gets prettier hour after hour.

Danielle Schilling, Hitchin, Hertfordshire

CORNISH STORMWATCH

Before that
Violent disturbance of the atmosphere,
Blackened granite earth falls silent.
The pockmarked bog is tattooist punctured
With blue volt colouring matter.
There is cloudburst percussion rudiments
On armadillo cairns.
Jamaica Inn barrel,
Becomes hollow hemisphere vessel
For Buddy Rich rain sticks.
Under novel-eyed scrutiny
Of Daphne du Maurier ghosts.
Pantheresque Bodmin beast claws,
Offer no crumbs of comfort
To lesser scavengers.
Amid pointed beak tor and burial chamber.
White chapel night cloak spectre,
Hovers over red-smeared lady dusk.
Writhing in the agony ague
Of angry knife blade thunder.

Paul Dunne, Stevenage, Hertfordshire

TEAM VICAR

The solemn season of Lent begins on Ash Wednesday
Would you please ensure that all artificial flowers and
wrapping are removed by this date.
Team Vicar and the Churchwardens.

Go Team Vicar! Do your thing!
Hark, the herald angels sing!
Meet the bishop, open fêtes,
fit us for the pearly gates.

Go Team Vicar! Ring those bells,
from Durham, Lincoln, Lichfield, Wells.
Marry chaps to girls they want
dunk the babies in the font.

Go Team Vicar. Rev the gas,
from morning to nunc dimmitis.
Help the poor, support the needy,
Succour both the ragged and tweedy.

Go Team Vicar! Here's the rub:
save us from Beelzebub.
And when our lives are at an end,
pray our souls to God will bend.

David King, Bramfield, Hertfordshire

THE STILL COLD LAND

Winter permeates the land,
In April the earth holds no warmth,
Ice forms in the bones
And the trees withhold their leaves.
Across the bare fields
The wind cuts like a knife.
Gnarled dead trees stand
Across the skyline,
Sentinels
Clad in rattling green armour,
Guardians of the lingering winter.

Jennifer Maskell Packer, Maidenhead, Berkshire

RENEWAL

kindred spirit
come laugh with me
and let our souls collide
for life is far too serious
and rules, too many abide
recapture now the spring we had
and loosen those autumn feet
to slip among the crocus buds
and absorb the heavenly scent
too flippant though you think me now
too careless in my mood
as life bursts out in song and dance
it's no time to be a prude
the sap is on the rise, my friend
the birdsong fills the sky
my feet are fleet as once they were
and there's a smile in the mind's eye

Kirsty Harrison, Binfield, Berkshire

LATE NIGHT STORE

It was long gone midnight and it was still raining
the dream was over.
Mary Antoinette now lived over
the local Co-op store just off the motorway
with buy one, get one free special offer on cakes
her, Louis, lost his head when he caught her
with another, and she lost hers, too.

Now boney as a Christmas Day turkey carcass
with the immense weight of days,
her daughter threw rocks at her sometimes,
and that didn't help.

Some days were better than others
as her benefits drip, was slowly ebbing
and with her age poking endlessly
living amongst the last remains of the family silver.
But worst of all was her soup
for it was full of tears
when she dreamed beyond the motorway.

Trevor James, Radley, Oxfordshire

SNAKELINES

Writing one night, I slacken in sleep,
my pen trails the page and tracing snaking lines
of ink on white; a woman's back,
pale against black, the shapely nest of hip
and bone, enamel skin and inky thigh,
bold and spare, she lies reposing on my sheet,
a mole upon her shin.

I would be this to you, my far off, sleeping love;
this image of desire in viper lines that coil around
a woman's winding forms;
I would be sinuous, spare and strange,
and rouse up your seducer's storm.

But lurking by will surely be,
that cool harpy, reality,
whose sneaky lamp reveals the fact;
the unsmooth back, the slackening,
and foils my reverie of snaky limb on limb.

If daring wins and I with you one morning lie,
by this you'll know that I gave in:
the vestige of a snake-mark
on my shin.

Charlotte Suthrell, Oxford, Oxfordshire

THE SNOW QUEEN

She loosed her hair upon the land
Wherein the snow is woven.
The crystal braid flows through her hand
Until the earth is frozen.
Where'er she treads her silver steps
a little death will follow, her face exquisite symmetry
Its countenance of sorrow.

John Lupton, Camberwell, Greater London

UNTITLED

Folk rock.
Cucumber sandwiches and brightly coloured eyeshadow.
Murder mystery reruns on a Sunday afternoon.
Walks in the park.
Raspberry vodka.
Wooden roses, scuffed old shoes,
Meaningful stares, given and received.
Elegant furniture with a distressed finish;
Dressers, chests of drawers.
Old stickers.
Creased love letters which achieve
Perfection through imperfection,
The feeling of the sun's rays on gently-browning skin.
Picket fences, gleaming white window panes,
Handfuls of fresh, moist soil, thrown into the air.
But most of all my boy,
Oh how I do love my boy.

Ruth Kurowski, Egham, Surrey

RETICENT STAINS

All wounds will take a while in time to heal
Soon nature's blessing will erase the pain,
Except for one no cure can ever seal
Which stays an open, lifelong, fractured vein.

Yet, from this secret artery the world denies,
Love's arrow makes words immortal spill
Invisible to sense, whose mortal skin defies
The lifelong spell, which doctors cannot kill.

This silent wound whose every lovedrop stains
Moist pages of a dream recites an ode,
Which draws all memory the day sustains,
Coagulates drying in the dark's abode.

For every word which stains the silent page
Removes the name of death, age after age.

Criton Tomazos, Enfield, Greater London

GOODBYE KNACKERED BODY

Goodbye knackered body,
Good riddance, I say.

It held you back so many years.
A slow and painful prison for your soul.
It endured so much beyond its time
It kept you in,
It pinned you down.

So goodbye knackered body,
Good riddance,
You won't be missed.

But your soul,
How I do love and do so miss.

But be,
Go dance, run, fly, sing, be free.

Caroline Taylor, Ashford, Kent

TULIPS

Opalescent blue glass jar,
Standing in striking sunlight.
In deep, the green, green stems
Clustered with innumerable bubbles of air,
Each a gleaming prism, a mandala of light
Playing with reflections. Summer at last?

So, so hot, the blue belies the heat,
The colour of a fiery summer sky.
Yesterday, the buds were tight,
Smooth, latent lumps, singly lined.
Now open redder than a temper,
Flaunting the blue and kissing the heat.

Robert Newman, Haringey, Greater London

7PM

At the horizon, she waits
before her lover's milk rays
drench the leaves.

She is Eve's apple aglow.
Night coils around her
the sky is dotted with her blood.

She gives birth
to a twilight sieve, her daughters
Cassiopeia, Andromeda.

Earth holds its breath.

Sangita Konnur, Hendon, Greater London

I DON'T LIKE YOUR POEMS

I don't like your poems, she said
And that's when I knew it was dead
And she'd never seduce me
More likely refuse me
Because she didn't like what she read

I don't like the theme, she said
It's weak and it hangs by a thread
She pulled it apart
Like a knife through the heart
Then endeavoured to rip it to shreds

I don't like the flow, she said
And that's when it entered my head
That the words which I wrote
That I wore like a coat
Would never tempt her into bed

Pete Rigby, Belvedere, Kent

THE PITCH

They want lines of limited length,
you want freedom
and footsteps in the carpet
on lone rotten weekends,
I came upon this moment
time and time again.

The air was full of soaked insects
in sudden neon armament,
lines of passengers
in bustling economy,
passing by the rolling meats
lithe traffic
the echo of impatience.

The pulsing steps
and stentorian cabs
I came upon this moment,
time and time again.

Paul Cross, Romford, Essex

MIGRATION

A V-shaped regimental squad,
Equidistant, travelling in a line.
Hot pursuit flying tail-to-tail
Sanguine strings of silhouetted birds.

Direction changes. All must mix and match,
But keep together as a fluid form.
Stragglers rush to capture new design,
Gull guaranteed to make the perfect shape.

The lead usurped, all speed and alter course,
Those at the front must take command.
The sky possessed of frantic flock,
No longer clear expanse of quiet blue void.

A bird's eye view over fields and sand.
What sights of beauty theirs to view?
Where will their journey come to rest?
In foreign climes a home for winter warmth.

Jill Wright, Frinton-on-Sea, Essex

TO A BUTTERFLY

Where is the nettle leaf supporting you
Showing your speckled wings in natural view?
Close by the woodland? In the peaceful glade?
Or in the country cottage garden shade?

Or in the picture in the gallery?
Or in the wanderer's poetic memory?
Now here the nettle holds you close in my
Emotions never stung, my butterfly.

Robert Martin, Canterbury, Kent

THE RIVER WALK

How many times have we walked these river banks
You and I, lost in each other's company
As the passing tableau of life
Goes by on the river?

Every time is different.
Sometimes, there are solitary rowers
Or pleasure cruisers full of day trippers
There are swans and ducks
And people walking their dogs along the towpath.

On sunny days people sit outside
The café while the children run and play
And on cold wintry days only the
Brave venture forth leaving the river to us alone.

Janette Patterson, Isleworth, Greater London

LUST

It wasn't what he said
It was the way he said it!
His swollen male ego bursting forth
In a flood of ejaculated
Cockiness.
He, who had jumped all
Macho man, between my sheets
For half a year or more,
Now wants me out!
Well, he's welcome to his new amour.
I hope he gets all clapped out
With his newfound concubine,
Because she's graced most beds
In her time. And when she
Tells him *out*, he'll shrivel up
And hang around feeling
Limp and useless. And he will care
What she says, and not the way
She says it!

Aleene Hatchard, Brentwood, Essex

THE BOOK OF LOVE

We found the book of love once
Do you remember when we opened its pages?
The dreams we had?
The plans we made?
Your hair was as dark as the night
And your eyes consumed my soul,
Your kisses whispered eternity
Embracing me in a citadel of immortality.

What happened to that book?
It must be hidden under a catalogue
Of missed opportunities
Of selfish thoughts
And apathy.

Help me search for that book again,
I know we will recognise it
For although the cover may be dusty
And worn with age,
The words inside will not have changed.

Peter Woodgate, Chelmsford, Essex

REMEDY FOR THE FRIGHTENED
(After Tony Curtis)

They arrive, cowering amongst the trees,
Emerging from the darkness
As shadows into the clearing.

I take a plume of quaking grass
I take a new beech leaf, brilliant green.
I take the gleam of light on the sea
I take a thrush's song at dawn.
I take sunlight on cold winter skin
I take stars on a clear, frosty night.
I take the marsh bathed in moonlight
I take rushes by the water.

I gather them into my arms
And bless them with my breath.
The frightened breathe in
and in
and in
And their fears drop away.

Zoe Brown, Uckfield, Sussex

HEART, MIND AND SOUL

An empty dwelling
Seeping with loss
Desiring to be filled

Controlled by a complex of mazes
Undiscovered realms hope to be found
Others are lost forever more

Tarnished but holy
Blessed with love from those that share its blood
The darkness still remains
Its purity denied by acts of man

Lewis Ikin, Bromley, Kent

IN IMITATION

Lo! Love, recall wherefore we firstly met
Steep'd in chaste summer's pleasant sadness,
That most unworthy reason freshly set,
Conceived barely in pregnant artlessness.
But then, departed and apart from thee
Thy face grew changed, in visage newly strange,
But beauty's stillness stayed my memory
Leaving love elsewhere than outlie plain;
For thy soul's substance mars or makes thy meat,
Lending fair symmetry to feelings fine,
So when we wander midst the poet's feet
Find nowt but secrets in the fall and rise:
Where doth the seat of love and beauty lie?
Who puts the question in mine April eye?

Alan Nash, Dartford, Kent

SO SAID THE SAGE HIPPOCRATES
TO ALL THOSE IN HIS CARE

If you take a gentle wander
through my airy tunnelled glade
you will hear the whispered voices
of my helpers' soothing aims

You'll soon be on the mend, they'll say
and with a slower, gentler pace
you'll imbibe the sacred herbals
from our calming womb-like cave

Your strength will slowly grow again
as will your sunshined glow regain
you're on the way to suppleness of limb
because we're vowed to heal and not to kill

Besides, this golden oil of flax
will be a wondrous source
of happiness and health
of energy and memory to make you smile

Already you look better, brighter
and less pale, so take the golden phial.
Our great physician in his trials
has found it beneficial to both man and child.

Rosemary Keith, Twineham, Sussex

HOW SOLID IS THE DREAM

All that came before these ruins on that ancient ground
Was clean and pure,
Unlimited and free
And connected to infinity.

And then outside and all around
The shades created from the dark
That limited and bound
The things we see
Replaced the silence with a dreadful sound.

The darker shades of light
Are not the lighter shades of night?
Though sometimes it may seem.

We only know within the shapes it makes
How solid is the dream
And what it takes to break.

Nicholas Kelly, Eastbourne, Sussex

STILL LIFE

She placed the potato on a blue sheet of paper
Giving her artistic thoughts of earth and sky,
There was only concrete beneath her flat window.
Holding it, she let her hands explore its shape,
Unwashed, the powdery soil dusted her fingers.
For the best light to fall across its skin
She turned the potato this way and that.
Oils, watercolours, pastels, pencil,
How best to portray in still life this popular vegetable.
Oh, to hell with it, she said,
I'm going to have chips.

Angela Higson, Westminster, Greater London

THE DRINKING EXERCISE

And once or twice within the bars
I drink alone, whenever
I watch the pub through empty halves
and people seem together.

And once again within my bars,
I'm not alone, however,
the empty half is watching me
like I had drunk forever.

And once before I brought my friends
and wasn't that a laugh,
we smashed the bars within ourself
and emptied our full half.

Peter Goodchild, Hammersmith, Greater London

TWENTY TWO FLOORS UP

The lift grinds and shudders to the top; stops.
Doors stammer, slide apart.
Two flights of stairs wind up to the roof,
My legs tremble with the strain
Below me cars and people,
Rushing, crushing, causing pain.

From here, they're just dots, a moving pattern
There's the park, swings and roundabouts catch my eye.
Children zig-zag, spin and fly.
Swans glide across the pond, ducks dibble upended,
The geese just squat and scowl.

Office blocks rear up, concrete and steel.
I watch the march of the masses
Weekend dreaming, work bound.
I hear trains clang and shunt. Where do they go?
I don't know - to and fro? Round and round?

I drink some wine, Chardonnay
I float, I drift, I gaze at the sky.
Soon I shall return down to earth, into the fray.
Can't wait. I'll go straight away
Look out world, here I come.

Carole Carlini, Bexhill, Sussex

TO JESSICA

The towpath reveals its catch for the day
Mud and driftwood starts to decay
Spirit of my mother
Comfortable in her chair.

Dappled, the moving reflections
On the walls about her.
Quacking ducks and wheeling gulls
The textured background noise
To her unaffected poise.

Brahms piano waltz
Reminds me of her
Her playing was gracious
And lacking in ego
A woman of refinement and taste.

In all the houses
Of my childhood, all three
Spirit of my mother
Dances there for me.

Ruth Strupinski, Richmond, Surrey

KIDS

The kids have gone to bed
The room's as still as a lake
The telly is showing that ad
Of the wonderful Copenhagen break.

Then some Lar-de-dah in a dog collar
Starts spouting out the screen
Telling me I'm going to be saved
By a man he's never seen.

The kids have gone to bed
They're tucked up safe and sound
I'm trying to unravel bank statements
But me head is spinning round.

She'd get at least fifty thousand
When the coffin lid closed on me face
Enough for an arse and tummy tuck
Plus the mortgage paid on this place.

The kids have gone to bed
They could go to Disneyland
Do they really need a dad
When a plastic mouse could hold their hand?

Keith Drake, New Malden, Surrey

SHADE OF DOUBT

We loved so much that any shade of doubt was death.
So I left you
and you left me
then I left you
until uncertainty was a blunt knife turning in the heart.
Will the last to leave please put out the light?
I was
I did
and we each lived ever after in the dark.

Sarah Maxwell, Mill Hill, Greater London

LAUREATE

Inside a London terminus
Stands he in hat and coat
Upon steam train and omnibus
His wistful thoughts would dote
Champion of railways
In slayer Beeching's time
Tranquil halcyon heydays
Immortal verse and rhyme.

Where shining track divided trees
To smoky towns beyond
Shrill whistle filled his summer breeze
With poignant memory fond
Oh bronze man of St Pancras
Wordsmith extraordinaire
Inspiration came to pass
The day I met you there.

John Byrne, Tooting, London

ARCHES

Upside down they trap the new-felt brine
And flourish in a city made of sulphur
Where lay the bones of old decisions
Where grapes hang dubiously by the wall
Green with the rain of earth-trapped lime.

So will these stones turn green in time
And lose their pale sharp edges in the night.
The walls lack voices down the echoing drift
To tell the nearby arches to be still
Whose echoes will resound across the rift
And down the alleys of the nearby street.

No man can know the truth
Which lies there
Behind that granite wall.
Only the arches hold the secrets
Of past voices, feet and songs.

Adrienne Mace, Croydon, Surrey

HOLY COW

What a tale I have to tell
You won't believe this thing
I was sitting at my desk
When a cow dropped in.

If you're wondering let me say
It was surprise I was feeling
It didn't knock at the door
Just dropped straight through the ceiling.

It landed on my desk in a
Shower, not of gold but of plaster
You always wonder how you'll cope
When confronted by disaster.

I'm proud to say I didn't panic
I sat back rigid in my chair
Idly wondering if this counted
For insurance as normal wear and tear.

Gillian Harris, Guildford, Surrey

SUMMER WEDDING

Orion points the way back to the moon
Gentling itself above the distant cliffs
Between the lines of cloud which all too soon
Will drift and spoil the moment, as it sifts
The softness, trailing pools of light
Across the fields. Inside the barn a dance
To celebrate another wedding, bright
With expectation, casts a glance
Of distant shadows spinning round the yard,
Where laughter and familiar conversation
Smudge the night, easing out the hard
And edgy silence into a muted fusion
Of faith and hope for what was promised here
That love may last as long as stars appear.

Brian Hick, St Leonards-on-Sea, Sussex

WAITING

I sat and watched the water's edge
I sat and looked for you
I watched the water ebb and flow
Where you and I once stood

I hear your voice still in my head
Your laughter in the air
I feel your arms around my waist
As we dance then dance again

Now I sit alone at the water's edge
I sit and think of you
For though I know you're truly gone
I'll always wait for you

Nicola Williamson, Oxted, Surrey

POLYPHEMUS

In his one-eyed cogitations, he knew
he was only a farmer of mangy sheep,
resented by the landless yokels, who
kept plotting with a hostile god to keep

his island on the boil. His worried wife
warned him that this had brought along
some mainlander, reputed in his life
to be ambitious, super-cunning, strong

in argument and with no family
to tie him down. How could a local,
however big, compete? He tried muscle

which didn't work, waited dumbly
to be outclassed, caricatured by fame,
his eye burned out, and Nobody to blame.

Ron Taylor, Wimbledon, Greater London

APPOETITE

I love this world of wondrous words,
Delight in sampling savoury sounds,
A gourmet taking so many rounds
Of verbiage dressed and seasoned.

I like to linger long on lines,
Wallow in mellow allegories,
Hallowing callow old memories
In phrases pressed and reasoned.

Intoxicating syntax sips,
Snipped syncopations whisked to the lips,
Sweet syllabubbles' silky flow,
Alliterations lit to a glow,
Rhyming, ringing, throbbing or terse,
Pleasure-plethora's plum's the verse.

Frank Groszmann, Harrow, Greater London

EMBERS

Side by side,
they looked into the fire, it
flickering shadows
across their faces, throwing
noses into
sympathetic relief

Heat rises, hits them like
a heavy towel as they
poke furtively
at the dying embers

Paper is thrown in,
blackens like liquorice stalks
as it collapses in on itself,
crumpling

Eyes bright, they watch
until the acrid smoke stings
their eyes and
bites their throats.
Coughing, they retreat to the safety of
the sofa.

Keturah Civelek, Southwark, Greater London

EBB AND FLOW

Rise up
Fall down
Rise up
Fall down
It ebbs, and when it ebbs
It seems at last I'm cured.
Perhaps it was only a trick
Of my sick brain, perhaps
It's mere hypochondria,
A mountain from a molehill,
A passing, silly thing.
Why worry? Things will turn out
Just fine, in the end, until
I start to fall down again.

Alister Dodds, Brighton, Sussex

A NEW HOUSE

The house is but the skeleton of life,
An outline sketch of what might come to be,
A mute, dry scaffold for our hopes and plans,
A hollow mask that cannot feel or see.

The sinewed strength of family life will bind,
And muscular praise enfold, encourage, protect,
Allow the mind to fill with hopes and dreams,
Each separate part synaptically connect.

Then breathe throughout the oxygen of love,
So lifeless flesh will take on form and tone,
And, like Ezekiel's bones, will rise and stand,
To be a living body we call home.

Elizabeth Maltman, Orpington, Kent

POEM ABOUT THE SEA

Hues of aqua blue and green
Reigning supremely as the universal queen
Where you and sky merge to infinity
You'll be the wisest old sage to eternity

Sweet smelling mists fill the lungs
And cool breeze leaping to the sky in bounce
Stark calm as a breast-feeding mother
You can be swift and menacing like no other

Immense and contemptuous savage
The countless humans you have ravaged
Like a crazy-eyed hurricane blowing
Reflections of the sun and moon glowing

What omnipotent and indominable power.
Unbounded salt water pouncing hour by hour
Thunderous waves, leaping, darting, roaring.
Like a symphony when calm, so alluring.

What vast secrets you hold
Of unprocessed data of the entire world
Whether red sea, black sea or dead sea
They are of the original constituency.

Enid Rosemary Daley, Islington, Greater London

SUMMER SOUP

There is poetry in making soup,
Laying out carrots orange brushed
Many times wedded with black rings.
Tomatoes, split like pomegranates
Spilling their red beads.
White plump turnips, frozen with fear
From being plucked.

All bundle up to the tall celery,
Its back stringly yellow, cracks like a firework,
And smells of oceans.
Onions, whose warm autumn coats stripped
Reveal silken wetness, and cause crying at their beauty.
And clever disguises.

Mushrooms lie startled and drunken,
Their little brown hats askew,
Showing veins weblike and multitudinous.
Soft and hand-made, like pintucks from Paris.
All cooked together, cause a glorious uproar.
A pot of delights; a perfume unmarketable
When they fuse into the poem of a summer soup.

Rosalind Berwald, Stanmore, Greater London

YOU'RE SWEET

You will forget of course
Why struggle to remember
The annoyance of a pain
An itch to whack, save its silence
You barely knew me so
It will be easy to pretend
Oh, but he was just a friend, I
Never really knew him in the end
Who? As the years clock by
But I will remember
For it is my way and
Count each second until that day
For it will come, chance and accident
Thrown together spinning out of silence
The whirl of the day and
What will you say as I ask you to stay?
That it is too late, that we are too poor
That all is lost in the folds of time, or
Laugh and call me sweet, though you are less so
And then walk on, down the street

Henry James Wood, Westcliff-on-Sea, Essex

TEASING GEORGIA

A rose is just a flower an indifferent person said
Clearly, they hadn't seen Georgia peeping from her bed
Yellow petals glowing, a velvet curling head
They'll grow and reappear again,
Every year once they are shed.

Sweet and softly perfumed, Georgia's fragrance entices
It is reminiscent of fresh and delicate spices
In the gentle morning dew she stands-out alone
A beauty, doubtless, when in bud,
But imagine her full grown.

As Georgia coyly tilts her head
All eyes turn in that direction
Rarely having viewed before such natural perfection
See her shyly nestle, before the wind compels a dance
But as she's strong, though graceful,
Nothing's left to chance.

Listen to her whispering in the gentle breeze
With every move she seems to talk, just rustling her leaves
Dressed in skirts of layered silk her aim is but to please
Until she shows her thorns because Georgia's just a tease.

Charmaine Fletcher, Basildon, Essex

South
West

DARTMOOR SUNSET

On Dartmoor, the sky is lemon
Edged with dove-grey waves
Of Cornish hills
Each with a glittering eye:
The lights of hidden homes.

Lynn Parr, Looe, Cornwall

LOVE'S DESPAIR

My love is like a dying flame
Lost in dark and gloom
Desperate for light
Sealed inside a tomb
Living there forever
For my heart a thorn
All the years to come
All the years to mourn
Now there is a river
Of memory and pain
You were right, nobody wins
Such a stupid game

My life is like a cloak of time
Wrapped around a frame
An empty, cold, unhappy soul
Blind and deaf and lame
Everything and nothing
Nobody and all
If only death would call

Jeanne Bradley, Torquay, Devon

EXILE

I have come here too late.
There is no room in the coffin of my destiny
for that other life.
The past, impoverished years
rage back at me.
Empty-handed I travelled them,
giving nothing to enrich their aridity.

Now I am depleted by my fears.
Now, when I most want to stay,
I must walk away.
There is no home for the exile,
no belonging for the dispossessed.

The falsehood of memory
is all I have left to cherish.
The past, that is not past, still vibrates,
wrapped around recycled emotions.
But what price is to be paid
for the integrity of dreams?
Lonely laughter, resonating silences,
no one to cry for.

Indranee de Silva, Frome, Somerset

FIELDS

I long to run my fingers
through a meadow's matted mane;
through tangled vetch and buttercups,
scarlet pimpernel, vervain.

I long to scuff my sandals
in heaps of scented grass,
weaving strands between my toes,
pollen-dusted as I pass.

I long to lie and cloud-watch
under heavy hawthorn trees
that shake their petals on my head,
irritated by the breeze.

I long to sit and listen
to the chitter of a mouse
or far-up cadences of larks
and far-off mournful croon of cows.

The metro shakes my high rise.
Planes roar up above.
But in the crib of memory
I nurse the meadows that I love.

Gillian Minter, Chippenham, Witlshire

THE WAITING GAME

Light filters softly through my window, the clock
counts down incessantly. The breathy chill
of the wind touches my cheek. It will be soon.

I lie silently, drinking in the sounds around me;
gentle hum of the machines like bumblebees,
distant chatter, animals at the watering hole.

The light makes patterns on the sheets, I stare
at the sun until it sears my eyes orange. Until
all I can see is the light and those I have kept waiting.

Sofy Bevan, Gloucester, Gloucestershire

BEAST OF EXMOOR

Staring with golden-yellow eyes ablaze,
they seem to burn a hole right through
me. Jet black, cat like, but with rounded
not pointed ears. He turns to streak away.
Panther or Puma, I wonder.

Around me the moors seem to glower.
Heavy grey clouds dip down and hold the
threat of rain. While low light slants across
the valley. Gorse flower spikes stand above
purple patches of heather.

The ancient hills roll away, stone strewn paths
cut through dark brown bracken. Then I hear a
clap of thunder, crashing and crackling, before
a fork of lightning splits the sky. Transfixed, I
feel first drops of rain as the heavens open.

Frances Lowe, Bridgwater, Somerset

WIFE DRIVING

Death hurtles towards my life,
a small car driven by my wife.
Roadkill, I line up my snout and await
your urgent delivery of fate.

However uncertain your arrival seems
you will devour these English fields
and tender towns, you've no time to admire
each barren village and godless spire
carefully traced by your forefinger that lies
on the route unfolded between your thighs,
veins turn to arteries, blue and wide,
speed cameras look away.

For all they can do is report what was once,
not tell who it is whose time has come.
A confetti of speeding tickets fall to the floor,
startled, I reach for the door.

Mark Wynne, Westbury, Wiltshire

FLOWERS OF THE TARMAC

Where are the flowers of the tarmac, Ma?
I can't see them from where we are.

The tin cans roll when the town-winds blow,
Crisp bags and plastic bags toss on the flow,
Grey gobs of chewing gum spittle the ground,
Fag ends and sweet wrappers surface bound.

See that child happily swinging,
Joyful tumble of smooth slide flinging,
Scrambling ladders to a playhouse den,
Elegantly scripted with moorish pen.

Rivals with twig-swords, a water gun,
A starfish cartwheel graciously spun,
A brood jogs a supermarket trolley trundle,
To untamed yells of a playfight bundle.

Why are you telling me about them, Ma?
Because that's where the flowers of the tarmac are.

Lesley Bairstow, Marlborough, Wiltshire

ANNIVERSARY PHOTOGRAPH

Sepia background, smudged black figures
Held rigid in time.

He stands, guardsman straight, ramrod straight,
Moustaches twitching.
She relaxes in chair, at ease, despite fixity of pose,
Bouquet of roses, lightly clasped, on her lap.

Her eyes twinkle. Her kindly mouth,
Though severely set in straight line, smiles.
Clumsy boots in no way diminish her grace.
Black dress, pearl necklace stark against its severity,
Age her before her time.

Hello, grandma. Sorry I never knew you.
Happy twenty-fifth anniversary.
She nods.
Hello, granddaughter.
I would have surrounded you with my love
As I did all my family.

Granddad stands protectively behind her chair.
I picture scarlet tunic overlaying black,
A relieving splash of colour.

Judith Marr, Weston-super-Mare, Somerset

FATHER'S DAY

What can we give him for father's day?
We've exhausted ties and socks,
And even last year's cufflinks,
Are still snug inside their box.

There's no room now for more CDs
For books, there's no more space,
Handkerchiefs and aftershave,
Have in turn all had their place.

We've bought him tools in days gone by,
But DIY has lost its clout,
It's feet up in his armchair now,
So even slippers don't wear out.

I said *Let's ask him what he'd like*,
That nearly caused a riot,
But then, I asked him anyway,
He said *Just give me peace and quiet.*

Joan Knight, Portishead, Somerset

TRAVELLING

The train clunks and grumbles into action,
The floor is black as diesel with a hundred footprints,
The seats are ripe and my table disintegrated long ago.

The old lady sneezes over her scotch egg and weak tea,
A sad old farmhouse that has forgotten the sounds of life,
Sits uncomfortably in a forest of nettles.

We grind to a halt,
The old lady steps out gingerly, showing white knees.
Engines meet and shudder, whistles blow, guards run.

It is unlikely I'll make my connection,
I am transported not to my destination,
But back in time.

Marnie Ellis, Wells, Somerset

LAMENT OF THE UNTATTOOED LADY

I sat beside you last night
making witty conversation,
when I physically ached
to take off my glasses
and remove your clothes.
To take off your glasses
and remove my clothes.
To feel your hard muscles
taut against my yielding
flesh, then you said that
you liked women with tattoos
and all that I can offer
are voluptuous stretch marks.

Joy Edwards, Bradninch, Devon

INTO THE NIGHT

You slipped away into the night
That starry, wondrous, cool clear night
Where beauty storms to match your soul
And I stand alone and seem to die
The voice of fragrance now gone
I turn to saddened footsteps walk
Where no beauty stays to share the night
The tears are warm but painfully bled
And in mares and dreams here in my bed
I search and ask for a reason why
That this love I have, I must always hide
But who knows? Perhaps in eternity
With Him as witness for all to see
I like a plaintiff might state my case
Of this love for you with the smiling face

R T J Harris, Tiverton, Devon

HEROIC THING

My father did the heroic thing
For one so self-sufficient
So ungregarious that
He could count his friends on
The thumb of one hand -
Got married and had kids
"Got a life" as we say
He counselled me just the once
That I remember
Son, don't have bloody kids unless you are
Bloody desperate for 'em.
Now, half-my-life on
Devoid of desperation
I wonder what depths of discontent
Those twelve little words rose from
Did blank unself-awareness
Conspire with conformity
And my mother's winsome ways
To produce such a life without music
One long mistake?

John Rustage, Winchcombe, Gloucestershire

LETTERS OF DEMAND

The tentacles of duty thrust their way
Across the page,
Suckering words that drag the victim back
Into the cage.

The tentacles of love tap light their words
Along the singing sands of happiness and joy,
Soft tendrils beckon from afar
With promises of pleasurable ploy.

The tentacles of pity writhe
In darkening syllables of pain
And clamp their suckers deep
Into the heart and brain.

The words *I need you* look the same
Upon the written page,
But oh, how duty, love and pity shape
The choice between one's freedom and the cage.

Audrey Dowsett, Lechdale, Gloucestershire

BRANCHES OF SKY

You lie
Your head over mine. Your weight bearing down,
Entwined in an embrace with no escape.
Softly, slowly, you wrap around me
These branches of sky.

I smell pepper, spices, the essence of earth.
Red, green and gold.
Scents of an ancient world, a time when lions roared
Now no more.

I cry
Not for myself. Not for you.
I cry for the peace of the moment,
The dark stillness of calm.
Inside, deep inside, another listens and waits.
Their time now.

Katie Grant, Dorchester, Dorset

AFTERNOON IN CHELTENHAM

He cried silently,
Tears rolling down his face,
In a coffee shop in autumn.

He made light conversation,
Shared a joke about muddled orders.
Talked to a stranger
There is a shortage of sugar.

Time speeding by at a different level.
His car was still in the multi-storey,
Could be shut in for the night.

Mundane objects cleared his mind,
The rain-streaked sky brightened,
And the waitress caught up with herself.

A busy late afternoon
In Cheltenham.

Pamela Davies, Bournemouth, Dorset

INFINITY

Intrigued, I gaze in wonder at the sky,
A darkened void bedecked with countless jewels
Flung by the hand of God.
A myriad of secrets yet unknown,
Where time no longer plays a major part,
And distance forms immeasurable depths,
The glimpse of hope our comprehension taunts
As knowledge still unfathomed lies between.

When will the light break forth,
The truth unfold with mysteries explained,
Our restless spirit calmed, our fears subdued
As wisdom will become reality.
For dawn proclaims the rising of the sun,
Majestic noble landlord of the sky,
Evicted shadows flee, enlightenment appears
So answer now, what is my purpose here?

Dawn Cawley, Plymouth, Devon

THE CAMERA ALWAYS LIES

You become beautiful
when the camera flash
bleaches your skin
and your features dissolve
into pixels. In the instant of light
that stings your eyes,
all your flaws are blurred away.

Just your face left, the stark
imprint of black lashes
ringed by eyeshadow;
butterfly wing bruises
of frosted violet,
suggestion of a nose
and your smile,
a smear of colour.

You get red-eye,
but that's the price you pay
when you're only attractive
in technicolor.

Talitha Black, Bideford, Devon

DIG (FOR SEA, FOR LAND, FOR HOPE)

Should I dig some more of the earth today?
What shattered lighthouse bulb and what riches
should my shovel clank amongst the decay?
The brittle bones laid about in ditches
make each treasure I find more exciting
comparing it with the cracked skull I shook
in my cupped hands after Monday's digging,
or Tuesday's find of a fisherman's hook.
There's got to be an array of wonder
scattered below amongst the stinking dead,
If I just root underneath a shoulder
of a farmer's loved one who'd never wed.

I may find beauty and could sell my land,
move to the sea with five rings on each hand.

Richard Thomas, Totnes, Devon

PILGRIMAGE TO JOHN BETJEMAN'S GRAVE

To the right of the path and facing the sea,
Sheltered by tamarist lies ,John B.
The headstone, rather too ornate
But suitable, in local slate
Bears his legend and the date.
And there, with the sacred, the profane;
Hothouse crysanths in cellophane;
A pebble and some pinks, quite dead
Peculiar blessings on his head.
I wondered what he would have said.
I turned to go, and as I went
There sprang to mind *so kindly meant.*

Jo Heydon, Rock, Cornwall

TIME

I have wasted a lifetime of you.
Little did I the innocent know
how soon you would fast flow;
why did you not tell me so?

Would not a faithful friend
a subtle hint sooner send?
Luxuriantly lengthy, dreamy day;
endless, carefree, childhood play.
Such cunning artifice; (at the sweet cherry)
I would bite twice.

But no, the rehearsal is real
and I am brought to summary heal.
So much missed fun, and life left undone;
momentous matters to finish,
but you false friend my allotted span diminish,
for as I turned around
you cannot extra be found.

Now I rue my faith in you,
proudly in boasting prime
and me with so little time.

Elvena Grace, Sweetshouse, Cornwall

SAVIOUR OF JERSEY

Dissolving darkness, creeping light,
one frosty morning, brent geese take flight.
For Judas curses with pointing hand,
upon our shores, French soldiers will land.
Through low water gullies, past limpet covered rocks,
sleeping guards shall fail to spot.
A taciturn march in quiet streets, houses with
occupants, tranquillized by sleep.
Taken by surprise, witnesses fall in silence,
bayonets fatigued in cold bloody violence.
Capitulating governor, demands shall be met,
shameful victim of an idle threat.
A valiant major, mustering our troops,
disobeying orders, his men shall swoop.
Enthusiastic leadership, chasing away despair,
hearts filled with courage, French invaders beware.
Cannonade from muskets, shattering bones,
thoughts void of mercy, tormented groans.

Mutilating onslaught, French soldiers will succumb,
Major Peirson the hero, death of our glorious son.

Carl Michael Dowden, St Martin, Channel Islands

MIRRORS

The gnarled and wrinkled faces of our fellow men,
Are but a pale reflection of their accumulated toil.
The very particles of their being from time immemorial.
They show us their woes and sorrows,
Their lives of hardship, famine and sickness.

Every person alive today cannot know
The full history of their being,
Their genetic mix, their movements across continents.
The battles they fought, won and lost.
The daily struggles for survival amongst
Their family, tribe or nation.

Yet they are with us now, for long or short a span,
But that we could interpret their haunting faces and
Read them like a book.
And wonder, as St Paul once said, if that pale reflection
In a mirror will one day fade,
And we will see our maker, face to face.

Margaret Boden-Heaume, Guernsey, Channel Islands

FISHING FOR WORDS

Words shoal in the mind
and have to be fished for.
Familiar, everyday words
are easily hooked, caught
and thrown back, so that
they may grow bigger.

Elusive, silver-backed words
are far harder to catch:
they tip the float of memory,
twitch the line of recollection,
snatch the bait and are gone;
the ones that got away.

Anne Ashman, St Ann's Chapel, Cornwall

SHORELINE SHALLOW

As dancing silver spirits flecked water,
A blue heron stepped lithe and languid,
Encircling silver water spread circumferences.

Breezes rattled sharp green palm edges,
So frilled rippling shadows sketched
Hot fingers across white sand.

Folding the dagger of its wings
A pelican dived separating blue.
And a dancing spirit scribbled content across shallows.

Then,
I
In an almost stillness,
Left a footprint interloping into soliditude.

Trisha Driscoll, Polzeath, Cornwall

COLLIERS WAY

The track is no longer there
As the railway line has become a path
Following the old Somerset and Dorset way.
From Dundas Aqueduct to Frome
The smoky and dirty trains
Rattled over bridges and through tunnels.
It is quiet now, just the cluck of pheasants
Prowling in the woods, cleaved
In two by tarmac.

Nature is reclaiming her own with trees
Advancing, overhanging, and dripping with rain.
The stomp of my boots splashing
Through puddles on the path.
Hard to imagine the noise of mining,
Colliers walking wearily to work,
Horses pulling carts of coal.
They named it Colliers Way to remind us
Of forgotten feet that passed this way.

Susan Coles, Bath, Somerset

East
Anglia

THE LEAVES OF LOVE

Twirl and tumble, twist and twine -
Cascading, fragile leaves,
As autumn dexterously her russet
Tapestry now weaves.
Alas! These brittle souvenirs
Of summer's vanished day
Like vestiges of clinging love
Must wither and decay.
Though winter cast a fluence bleak
And chill upon the earth,
The branches bare and lonely hold
The secret of new birth.
And time can to a heart bowed down
By grief new stirrings bring;
Burgeon, blossom, bud and bloom -
The leaves of love's bright spring.

John Harris, Heacham, Norfolk

AUTUMN'S HOMEWARD FLIGHT

Here slowly falls this autumn's twilight hour,
Embraced within her soft reflected light:
Whilst now the day's bright sun begins to wane,
And waters of the sea must fade from sight.

The pine trees, darkest green in silhouette;
The dusty purple clouds draw ever nigh;
The silver birches, each bedecked in gold;
Still yet, the day from darkness doth defy.

One ribboned beam of orange light does hold
Far out, along that margin, ever faint;
Such love, such power, unsettles heart and mind;
Once more, the Lord's almighty hand would paint.

The creek still glistens on in palest white,
And gently waving reeds breathe one last sigh;
Whilst high above, in heaven's vast endless space,
The ragged skeins of pinkfoot homeward fly.

Derek Lane, Peterborough, Cambridgeshire

ODE TO ELSIE

In a world of flux, you, my cat
are a rare constant.

The slightest encouragement
and you appear with an enquiring
Purrup?
Kneading intently with velvet paws,
slow push and pull
in time with the rising falling rhythm
of your geiger purr.

A syrupy blink and I swear a smile,
green-eyed gaze brimming with adoration.
I am your whole world
and not afraid to express your love
you roll with ridiculous abandon
and then mould, plump and warm,
to the curve of my knee.

In this world of flux,
you are my constant,
and I,
yours.

Nancy Stephenson, Cambridge, Cambridgeshire

WINTER

Tread winter with me,
Watch as the
Fingernail glitter moon
Slips silently behind cold clouds.
Cry frosted tears,
Remembering,
Forever remembering,
Autumn paradise.

Leila Anani, Debenham, Suffolk

SHE WAITS

Looking out the window, head
tilting back and forth
now and again on tiptoes
straining into the net
curtain, I imagine her furrowed brow
the brown spots in her eyes
flicking from side to side, fingers
leaving their dusty half-moons
on the wood. All I can see is her
ragged hair and apron strings
swaying, from the back window to the
front, ears peering like a cat. The tea
is in the oven, nearly four hours have gone
by, yet the birds still sing and the
dog watches the click of the phone -
her aching bones slotting into place.

Kate Buck, Diss, Norfolk

REMEMBER ME

Lush rolling Cambridgeshire countryside
Reflected in imprisoned eyes,
This husk that meant so much to me
Stared from a bed he would not leave.
Chalk white in dying interlude
Intrusive tubes grew part of you,
Stern machines seemed constant visitors
Metallic cold inquisitors.
Came flickering spark two cloudy eyes
As though death's shroud you recognised,
A cherished friend from a long cast dawn
When summer days were ever warm.
Willow on ball flew boundaries
For passing moment we both could see,
Came trace of smile two dry, parched lips
That ever in my cold heart lives.
There as the living met the dead
Remember me, you softly said,
There as a spirit rose and flew
Old friend I will remember you.

John Cates, Cambridge, Cambridgeshire

THE WANDERER

From my hill at morning, flowers bloomed among the
wheat.
Charmed by the blue of cornflowers,
The enchanted red of poppies,
"I'm coming," I cried. "Wait for me!" How fast I ran.
How deep I waded into the long fields.

Plunging between barleystalks,
Fingers sticky with fly-spittle,
I shrank from the fat buzz of bees
Gorged on sickly meadowsweet,
Turned my eyes from wasps
Gouging soft beetle underbellies,
Sidestepped the silent, blind heave of worms.

Now my arms grow weary from
Warding off spiked rye-heads.
Close above my head vines throttle the bearded wheat.
I cannot see blue cornflowers. I cannot find red poppies.
Foot-sore, I thrust through corn-stubble
Back to a barren hill.

Lenore Abraham, Cambridge, Cambridgeshire

A LONDON EYE

Soar high as a seagull
Over a capital city to
Marvel at man's invention
His many and varied works

Of vainglorious rivalry
In attempts to surpass
Our maker's creativity
As we slowly revolve.

Our only means to hand;
To modify earth's crust a bit
Sift glass from metal, quarry stone,
Axe rare woods, capture light

Providence may smile
After all, he provided volcano
Earthquake, wind and storm
To test their validity

Nicholas Hills, King's Lynn, Norfolk

AN EARLY MORNING WALK

It is strangely hushed in the woods
No birds calling the news of the day.
The early morning sun filters through the green leaves
Creating a mosaic of light and shade.
The ferns are shoulder high enclosing our space
A bee soundlessly searches the wild honeysuckle,
All is quiet.
My dog halts, one paw raised,
Desperate for a sound to chase.
She looks at me imploringly, confused by the silence.
Last autumn's leaves, now part of the forest floor
Soften our footsteps, we creep away
Lest we wake the trees.

Doreen Hale, Sheringham, Norfolk

SHINE

Shine as a source of endless light
whose rainbows of colours deter the night
where daydreams are gentle as doves in flight
and sleep the sleep of angels.

Shine like a shower of soft moonbeams
inhabit the sea of a thousand dreams
where laughter and love are the timeless themes
and sleep the sleep of angels.

Shine like the sun in a golden sky
on warm, sultry evenings, a fragrance, a sigh,
an echo of summer, as life passes by,
and sleep the sleep of angels.

Greta Robinson, Ipswich, Suffolk

LISA

These autumn paths for me
will never be quite the same again:
for then you ran beside me,
your graceful form rippling in the sun,
and every now and then
you darted through the undergrowth
that bounds the well-trod lane
as something caught your eye -

And I
uncomplainingly awaited your return,
gratefully feeling the sun warm upon my back.

Yet now I lack your company and fun,
I know that someday soon
I shall tread these paths again
and another graceful form will run
darting to and fro,
teasing my love and I as we go
hand in hand along the well-trod lane
together making memories -
and are no longer sad.

Marilyn Lyne, Hadleigh, Suffolk

East
Midlands

SORROW

Rain,
Silver needles of sorrow,
Gleaming morosely in the tormented night
Life has shed a tear
And love lies weeping in the shadows
Forlornly mourning
Days gone by.

Janice Taylor, Ripley, Derbyshire

TIME

Weathered tombstone
Lichen covered
Who lay alone
Once loved and mothered?

Cold, stone, sober, grey
Encrusted white and mustard.
Tilting now, as if to pray
Whose inscription once shone gold and lustred.

Uptight memorial to him, to her
This polished slab erected.
Time and elements concur
To crumble, overgrow, leave dejected.

From womb to tomb
Time takes control
For bone and stone
He takes his toll.

Gillian Hartley, Repton, Derbyshire

WHAT IS LIFE?

Life is the gossamer thread -
A spider's web in action,
Interweaving its tendrils
Around the soul of man.

Creeping through the ages -
Tightening its hold,
Binding its victims of fate fast
To its core.
Clasping a lover's knot -
A newborn baby's cry,
Waiting in the wings
For the old man to die.

Through time and evolution
An intricate pattern winds
The tenacity to grip onto youth,
The call of wisdom beckons.
Knowledge beyond the meaning,
The force that beyond the heart's door
A wistful wish of breathing,
Truth, once more.

Mo Ward, Hinckley, Leicestershire

'OME!

The coal-hole cavalry advances,
Heads and shoulders bobbing over the brow,
Steel-segged boots striking sparks behind the rise.

Once-best jackets march abreast,
Baggy-elbowed, saggy-pocketed,
Atop work-moulded trousers, belt and string buttressed,
While steel-capped, battle-scarred boots
Complete the uniform
Of these hardy combatants, close comraded,
Whose weary arms swing spent ammo-case snap tins.

Coal-red wounds of mouths split and gape,
Grinning responses to red-rimmed whites of eyes,
As blackened faces mouth, "Tarrah,"
Deserting into the backs at each row-end.

While we scouts,
In shrivelled-up cardies and passed on shoes,
Pleased at the approach of tea,
Scatter through the brick-yard and into the scullery,
"Mam, me dad's 'ome!"

Eileen Wale, Selston, Nottinghamshire

TATTOO

The stinging, the pleasant pain
This act has made art remain
Hidden away or revealed
Forever there, never healed.

The wanting, the obsession
Prepare for your first session
Choose wisely or you'll regret
Are you ready? Not quite yet.

Natalie Beck, Heanor, Derbyshire

FEMINISTS CALL ME REGRESSIVE

I should have swung my sweet moon breasts
dripping with milk, staining the silk.
Should have dug in my nails, chewed to the quick
as I smiled and smiled across the MD's desk.
But he was expecting my productivity
before I was expecting you.
So I teetered on the brink of my high-heeled shoes
and let the fat cats suckle on my creativity.

Nappies I bought were changed by a stranger,
first words noted, but moments forever lost.
Mornings of clinging and brimming with loss,
evenings of guilt, strangled with anger.
Feminists may laugh at the call of my womb
but my suit doesn't warm in this empty tomb.

Trudi Macagnino, Southwell, Nottinghamshire

A PICTURE OF YOUR LIFE

Take a picture of your life
Hold it in your hand
Tread softly on the richest part
Ignore the barren land

Creeping softly through the warmth
You find the shadow of a smile
Let it stay amongst your thoughts
Consider it for a while

Some part you want to paint again
The blackness of despair
Wipe it out, renew with hope
Leave no futility there

You find a tangled mass of days
Growing in your healthy wood
Uproot the sorrow of the words
Leaving nothing there but good

When you have delved in every wood
Searched every path for strife
Return the picture to its place
The picture of your life

Jackie Heald, Wellingborough, Northamptonshire

FREEPARTY BLISS

The empty corrugated prefabrication vibrates, echoes
Sick resonance, booms, rips, cracks and low bellows
Feet stomp, heads nod, all bones below can hardly shake
Twenty five thousand watts of sound busting an
earthquake.
Bins and tops stacked high, bound by the crank strap
Ravers jump as the volume rises, daring to snap.
Elbows up, eyes wide, backpack bouncing all about,
Teeth grinding, jeans falling, let your arse hang out.
Kaleidoscopic colours of London's dawn twilight
Spring through the morrow
With sound creatures of the night.
Slip, slide, bump, grind, fall in squat juice,
Ah well, never mind.
Dogs scrounging, people falling,
Mash up ket heads simply stalling
Jumping, barging, noz balloon gassers recharging
Dj's seismic needles monitor the quake, still enlarging.
Hood taggin', fiends baggin', nutters dancin'
Heads stuck in speakers, the wasted now fallin;
Anything goes bruv, just leave out the brawlin'
Party in peace with warehouse vibes of London east.

Richard Savage, Long Eaton, Nottinghamshire

A MAUDLIN SOIREE

She strains for the sky,
And the dark whisky bottle;
Lights a cigarette
And lays the table for two.
The second chair will sit
Vacant
As the evening draws on,
So she plays a vinyl record,
And circles the room,
Spinning
And tripping
By the light
Of the gloom.

Lauren Hall, Sudbrooke, Lincolnshire

A SOLDIER DREAMS

Alone she walked, a child of magic night
Beside still lakes which mirrored starlight's glow
Cloaked only by the moon's pale silver light.
Dawn broke and night's sweet pleasures swiftly go
Eyes open ready for the hellish morn
Fleeting dreams of sweet skyclad maidens fade
Gone, in a blink, as if they'd ne'er been born.
Hasting hence, a trick my tired brain had played.
I prayed that I would one day meet her grace
Just hold her in my arms and smell her hair
Knowing her love my fear I'd boldly face
Lonely and cold like my foe over there.

Men facing death need loving dreams like this
Need to remember a sweet maiden's kiss.

Hugh Rogers, Scunthorpe, Lincolnshire

CALIBAN'S ISLE

Sun settles, the shadows gather in the park,
bringing darkness with them. Dawn reveals
their passing, the usual litter of summer nights.
Caliban rules this septic isle, these his whelps,
spawn of the vile, the beast visible,
marked with weakness, marked with woe, come to swill,
shriek, couple in vulgar pastoral. How sing this obscene
unpleasant land, hopeless, inglorious, drunk, uproarious?
How sing pastures green where trees fly plastic bag flags,
grass blooms beer cans, condoms, needles,
as a kingfisher perches on the trolley in the dyke?
Jerusalem builded here, graffiti pocked and pitbull packs
hunt, snap, snarl, prowling alleys and back streets,
claws to catch, ready to rip innocence
caught at bay by the bins behind the shops.
The shaven-headed smiler with the knife, tattooed ruffian,
waits in the shadows under the stair amid the fragrance
of urine, vomit, butt ends. Quomodo cantabimus?
Ah, Master Byrd, we are in rats alley.
Descant that to the sounds of broken glass.

Keith Linley, Lincoln, Lincolnshire

TRUTH

Wisdom
scribbled in chalk, canal-side veracity, flourishing
with weeded growth's tenacity, nourishing
new lives for old, raucous voices, city choices,
echo loud and bold.

Words
adorning wire and fence by field and wood and moor,
Keep Out, Private, Trespassers Will ...
threaten, bluster, warn, but make no sense,
where freedom beckons on the hill.

Trust,
designs in ink in childhood's pocket, whorls and whirls
and circled thoughts, brain engendered,
engineered, your secret,
if we could unlock it, of you and how you search and think,
for patterns shatter, patterns break.

Truth
daubed in paint by urban youth, brushed brashly
over a faded palimpsest on inner-city walls.
Players in the half-light, modern voices ask
how much more can you take?

Tina Negus, Grantham, Lincolnshire

SUMMER

Mixing our own medicines and dancing to the obscure,
Playing music with the cutlery,
eating mushrooms off the kitchen floor
and grapes from the walls.

The sun is shining and the wine is good.

Abandon your shoes, feel the grass between your toes.
We wander to the pond where the teacups grow
And leap through smoke rings until we fall
Asleep on the beach, tempting the rising tide.

Charlotte Hoare, Lincoln, Lincolnshire

FIFTY

Ten years ago
A lover told me
When you get to fifty
You'll give up sex for gardening.
That's what all women do.
Never, I panted, as the sweat dried.
Not I.

I did not know
That was a swan song.
Today
Nettles hurl their passionate darts
Jilted sparrows gasp for love
Brambles call me back
For one last embrace.
At night I turn my shoulder and sleep
Worn out by the hurly-burly
Of spring.

Alison Fairchild, Horncastle, Lincolnshire

AFTER RAIN

We drove home after rain.

The tarmac shone
with silver puddled patches.
In the lane, new laid hedgerows
threw long shadows
like spectres in our path.
Taking the drive towards the house,
low late sun back-lit
our line of slender birch
laying a giant cattle grid
across the track.

Gravel at the front door
still held pools of water
glinting with light.
There was no rush to go inside.
Leaning on the car
we just enjoyed
the reflected double arch
of the encircling rainbow.

Heather Chandler, Ashby-de-la-Zouch, Leicestershire

THOUGHTS ON A GREY, MAY DAY

If life somehow changes, and now you're alone
And loneliness beckons, no fault of your own.
Can one recapture that remembered way
That you once were, before today?

If you're suddenly there, out on that limb,
Clinging tightly, while your future looks grim.
You soon accept that the world and his wife
Have left you behind, content with their life.

If you find, when living this life alone,
Each dawning day seems an empty zone.
Try to welcome them in some worthwhile way,
Or you'll regretfully find you've wished them away.

If you mope around, feeling sorry for yourself,
It's undoubtedly futile, (you remain on the shelf)
To discover someone in like situation,
Would seem to be one's best expectation.

If I'm difficult to get on with, as some say, of course,
There's scant hope for me, I've flogged that dead horse!
No long lost friend will arrive from the past
To remember those good times we knew couldn't last.

Ena Swain, Loughborough, Leicestershire

DREAMING OF YOU

In the night I'll lift you sleeping
to dance with me upon the sky.
An owl will wake you from your dreaming,
Rising on a wind we'll fly.
The moon will dress you with her aura
Shining rainbows onto you
And I will kiss you with my promise
Now and ever, old and new
That I will always, always love you
Faithful, passionate and true.

Richard Hulett, Kettering, Northamptonshire

GOODBYE MY FATHER

Quiet whispers bathe my troubled soul
Flooding the void of physical being
Chances missed to touch, speak or hold
Only time can begin the healing

Weary muscles cloak fragile bone
A battle lost against the enemy within
Fought with valour by you alone
Your pure new life to soon begin

I call to you through silent voice
Invade my thoughts and comfort me
The space that's left was your own choice
You shed the body that set you free

Your spirit glides through endless light
And scented meadows on your journey
I feel your presence close at night
Now my love must set you free

Carol Tilley, Ilkeston, Derbyshire

FAREWELL TO BERWICK

Listening to music
my last days in Berwick
drift,
a tide of nostalgic reflection
bringing to mind
brisk walks on beaches
at sheltering places,
Berwick, Goswick
where Vikings had been before.
Here my ship landed
for this brief respite.
Coming to the service
for the last time
I remember the dead
those who smiled
or grimaced at morning worship
gaining what nourishment they could
from the broken world.

Rodney Ward, Chesterfield, Derbyshire

TIME

To this brown earth,
our bed of life,
I set out one seed to grow tall and strong.
In hope,
that I may watch it caress,
the highest cloud on a timeless day.

And perhaps,
as the mighty canopy unfolds,
in myriad tribes of calming peaceful green,
I will rest awhile beneath,
in this solitary spot we share.

To celebrate,
a love,
a life.
And glory in the moment.

James Hawkins Woodward, Lullington, Derbyshire

THE OPTIMIST DEFIED

When optimism rears its head
And rouses slumbering hope from bed,
When favourable expectation abounds
And desire dares to dream faith found,
When spring provokes such seeds you sow
Remember,
Little acorns from great oaks do grow.

Alan Robinson, Warnall, Nottinghamshire

BARN OWL

May, when nights come late
and waking dreams turn you out
I catch you gathering the twilight hour,
gliding over the rolling level,
where whitewashed hawthorn
frames the farmer's field.

Whirling, swirling, striding higher,
white strokes sifting the steady air.
Shaking sleeves. Undressing.
Splitting wings for a feast of things.
Ascending.
Plummeting.
Returning to those downy cheeks
where you once began.

Is it hard to stop the rivalry
for the delicacy of the rodent's tail?

Monica Norgate, Oakham, Rutland

West
Midlands

FEATHERS

This desire is stuck in a rut,
This stinging cut,
Won't stop bleeding though it's only a scratch,
Red with the urge to overwhelm you.
Yes, I have been foolish,
And I must confess,
I have fallen in love with my loneliness,
Ashamed at my lack of shamelessness.
Like feathers stroking glass,
I let the moment pass,
'Cause it's also soft,
Like the lips of a lover.
Wish to stop circling these cycles
And run for cover,
Safe in a place where a casual
Tilt of your chin,
Wouldn't knock me senseless,
And send my strength running,
I never saw you coming.

Lorna Meehan, Oldbury, West Midlands

TEMPTATION

Tempted to imbibe
Seeking the essence
That's none of the others;
Pouring and pouring
Drunk from pen's flow
The time slips away
The vessel re-fills -
Full until empty.

Sylvia Lees, Rugeley, Staffordshire

LOVE ON A SHOESTRING

My knees do not weaken for candles and roses.
They ache for daisies, plucked from gardens in the south,
carried in a tic tac box in an empty pocket,
a train ticket pinned to my wall to say
I was here. You did not dream me up.
When it's cold, I crave the scent of your neck,
and for you to brush my hair
as sleep climbs my legs.
Not sweat-laced satin sheets in five star hotels.
Not moonlit kisses in the rain.
If you were here, I would not need
to look, or touch.
I could sit in silence
and feel the hairs on your arm rise to meet mine
like the fingers of old, blind lovers
intertwining in the dark.

Bethan Ford-Williams, Walsall, West Midlands

SUBURBAN BUS SHELTER

10.05, 10.10, 10.35
Then every thirty minutes until 4 o'clock.
Bus times would seem to be ordained by God,
Framed in see-through plastic, grimed by fingertips.

Crisp packets shimmy in the fallen leaves,
Blown into corners with some dented cans.
A pair of trainers, laces tied,
Is caught upon the roof, just out of reach.

Graffiti decorate the chipped and fading paint,
Wayne4Jayne, then angrily scratched through, no more, no
more ...
Initials hacked by penknife in the wooden seat,
That boy's now seventeen and drives his mother's car.

The wind blows spiteful gusts of rain
As a scraggy cat slinks up and stops to sniff
A greasy paper bag, then saunters off.
A bus drives up, slows down, but doesn't stop.

Louise Henly, Wolverhampton, West Midlands

HOSPITAL SHOWER

The nurse was young and unimpressed
By the rapier-like scar from dewlap to paunch.
She disregarded my vulnerable nakedness
She was the professional, I was the patient
And she needed to supervise my showering.
Beneath the warm flow of water
I cleansed myself.
Holding the towel, she seemed detached
Adonis had left me some thirty years before
And Satyr had hidden himself in the undergrowth.
She proffered the towel maternally
And I was now a child having his Friday bath.
For a moment, I needed to be wrapped and embraced
And have the comfort of a bedtime story.

David Grayling, Leamington Spa, Warwickshire

FIREFLIES IN MY LAMPLIGHT

Fireflies in my lamplight,
Illuminate my hidden fantasies,
As bits of cotton and cloth float above its artificial flames
These broken bed springs and quilts sodden in sin,
Are glorified against this light which is softly,
Sweetly burning from outside and within
For I imagine you would look ever lush against
This backdrop of ecstasy.
It doesn't scream, demand and insult as we mortals do
No, this light is subtle in its wants and desires
In turn, leading me to be the obedient partner of you,
And it is because these emblems of magic
Are both artificial and non-existent
That I can keep you in my bed
With our shadows singing on the walls
And fireflies dancing above our heads

Victoria Maguire, Sutton Coldfield, West Midlands

A RESTING PLACE

You think there's no-one there:
wide fields across the gentle valley
where spring lambs call on the distant air,
smudged blue trees edge the horizon
beneath a pallid sky.

I am there,
my feet upon the grass of roughened ochre, coarser green
I watch the hedges brighten into summer,
the young wood warms its way to autumn.
I go to think, but only breathe, and be.

The landscape hides the footprints
of all passers by, but this is my seat, and my place.
Beneath this ground my parents' ashes lie, and I
sit here quietly while slow seasons soothe
my grieving with their passing.

Penelope Hewitt, Birmingham, West Midlands

THE GAME

A game, just a game
played by boys
lounging the summer through
in deckchairs, reading, sleeping
in clanging urgency, scrambling
engines firing
winging away, up, up
the nasal radio voice directing
toward fear, excitement, death
the few, fewer still, exhausted
in deckchairs, reading, sleeping
until the next time
a game, just a game
played by boys
the stake: a country's freedom
winner takes all.

Patrick Derwent, Kenilworth, Warwickshire

BELOW THE TINKERING TIN ROOF

Stormy grey clouds gather, ready to burst
The smouldering dense air high up above.
Cascading raindrops fall and fill the ground with
Pools of murky tears and smudge the colourful
Flower petals that were grown with love.
I sit and wait below the tinkering tin roof
For the watery waves to part and drink in every detail
As the sky becomes calm and light again.
Warm beams evaporate and slowly scorch the drying earth
And leave the dampness to linger a little longer.
I listen as the air is once again filled with sweet songs
And wonder whether the rain will come again.

Rosy Reilly, Bedworth, Warwickshire

HALF EXPECTING

Another spring emerging, and still you are gone.

Funeral white snowdrops push frail heads
towards a pale sun,
the bare earth below your memorial rose
terminally cold.

As if your voice could call to me,
as if I could find you in your knitting chair, the
agents of your cancer hidden in the wool basket,
underneath that last Arran sweater.

Walking in on quiet afternoons, you
sitting shadowed in the Marlow room,
medical science too late to save you.

Yesterday, your smallest grandchild had a birthday;
her thoughts full of the trampoline we bought her,
all attention centred on her own potential.

This morning,
strange that I woke early
head full of sharp images,
reaching out, half expecting
to see you there,
Mother.

William Joss, Whatcote, Warwickshire

CAFÉ AU LAIT

Metal against metal clanked his arrival
The hippity hop of uneven steps, yet
Regulated by the metal thud

Clambering through the winding
Timbered room, navigating a seated position

A work of art unrealised, until one foot
In front of the other is interrupted

Seated at his seat he awaits his
Daily café au lait

Hi George, they say
Same as usual then?

Nodding, his hands knuckle clenched
Around their metal companion
Waiting the signal to release

Grasping his cup of comfort

Laura Smith, Bulkington, Warwickshire

THE SALMON LEAP

I've seen men trawl
the mackerel seas for silver fish,
searching the shoals.
I've seen saints kneel
on golden knees, arms folded
searching for souls.
I've seen the power of the molten sun
I've seen the platinum moon
I've seen such things as men dread
in their secret dreams.
But beyond all these
is a holy thing I seek,
womankind is the song I sing
and for her men grow old and the salmon leap.

J R Heron, Newcastle-under-Lyme, Staffordshire

MINERAL ANTHOLOGY

A sentiment expressed precisely,
an itch, a wrinkle, an ache, a regret,
a critique,
a grumble, a resentment, a heartfelt moan,
an explosion of rage,
an observation bedecked with imagery:
any or all of these
but articulated carefully, skilfully yet unexpectedly,
with form, colour and texture
as in a collection of gemstones
from which, from time to time,
one can be selected
to be observed, handled, appreciated, admired
and given a loving polish.

Dave Brough, Southam, Warwickshire

MISBEHAVING

I want to really misbehave
but I'm not sure what to do.
I could smoke pot or dye my hair
a vivid shade of blue.

I could have a hot affair
and blame it on my age.
At least that's what my husband did
with his secretary, Paige.

I could stay out all night long,
get drunk down the old Queen Vic.
The kids can stay up for a change,
white-faced and worried sick.

I want my second childhood
to be more fun than my first.
I want to skip, play ball, climb trees
and blow bubbles, watch them burst.

My mum says it's perfectly normal,
just a phase I'm going through.
It'll soon pass so I should enjoy
misbehaving at age forty-two.

Tracy Davidson, Stratford-upon-Avon, Warwickshire

MICHAEL EAST

And I saw Michael East on Lichfield Green.
And where he walked the air disturbed, re-grown
Like many sweet scents from past gardens blown,
And spread wide, full as saints' calm eyes have seen.
The Bishop's dove-house in the setting sun
From long years called forth as fair song upgrows,
As Lord Paget's flock by Tusser's voice rose,
From The Age of Reason's death-grip fair-won.
What went you out to see? Ghosts of fair flocks?
Should Master East, a silhouette in spring,
Charm down the beams of sun and gladness bring
And full provide keys against demons' locks?
As they departed, Michael East and birds,
I sang as a dove-house choir these glad words.

Philip Williams, Cheslyn Hay, Staffordshire

AUTUMN

Swirling brightly coloured leaves,
The smell of the coming chill,
The brilliant sun no longer warms,
Trees begin to undress,
Their naked limbs waving in the wind.

The crunching sound of feet on leaves,
Smell the smoke of coal fires,
Sparkling frost lays on the ground,
Quietness,
Only the rustle of the leaves on the breeze.

These are the things that autumn brings,
The summer gone,
Winter is not far away,
How long will it be till spring?

Cindy Faulkner, Cannock, Staffordshire

A DEATH IN COMPUTER LAND

He died in the upstairs bedroom
By the light of the flickering screen
That showed his imminent bankruptcy
In columns of red, blue and green

Beside him the lonely keyboard
Lay silent and untried
For the fingers that would have played it
Were as dead as the circuits inside.

Did you see the downturn coming
Did you mark the shares as they fell?
As he planned a retirement in paradise
Did you book his ticket to hell?

Did you cry when you coolly told him
That all of his money was blown?
Did you drink with him to drown his tears
When his wife and his children had flown?

I blame not you but your maker
Who marked you damned from the start
When he gave you logic for emotion
And a silicon chip for a heart.

Simon H Lindley, Cheadle, Staffordshire

STOLEN AWAY

We know the Fey Folk change babies for their own
But who takes the old?
I sit with my mother
Holding her hand in her room
But inside she doesn't know me.

She keeps reading the same page
She keeps telling me about Auntie Jill
She keeps trying to go to work
I do not know this person
Who stole my mother?

Ian Ward, Wasall, Staffordshire

SPRING

I cannot see so clearly now
Now trees are in full leaf,
As when old winter's dripping boughs
Bowed down in stark relief.
This sorry sight was seen by all,
All sad, beyond belief,
Leaf filtered through these dappled screens,
Screens out the sharpest grief.

Where the litter of last year's leaves
Leaves thoughts of waste and spoil,
The humid balm of spring's return
Returns those leaves to soil.
With thoughts of those that gave me life
Lifeless in my heart,
As I respond to June's sun kiss,
Distress and sorrow part.

Jim Davies, Church Stretton, Shropshire

WIRELESS

Driven around the estate.
passing children and trees,
in a wash of afternoon light.

My laptop seeks networks
for access.
The sobriquets list
in the drop-down menu.

Barry, duck1066,
free4all, all locked out.

We pass pale bungalows
and I read Edna's Wireless Network.
Edna sits at her computer,
the grandson-given internet
at her marigold fingertips.

She occasionally dusts
this machine. Worried
to switch it on, as the webcam
might show the world
her threadbare dressing gown.

Alexander Ward, Stafford, Staffordshire

MADNESS AND MELANCHOLY

I did not know that life could be so at odds with me
That my mind could yield to madness.
I did not know that before my weary eyes
It could sting so much
And appear so black,
To a soul so lost,
To a soul so soft,
That this reality cuts and wounds with its hardness.
Oh how ill I feel in both body and mind,
And oh how sick I feel inside because of this world,
And what a bitter taste I have in my soul because of my life
That I feel like vomiting up my spirit.

Ian Michael Duncan, Oswestry, Shropshire

DERELICT BUILDING

Broken windows reflecting,
Deflected,
In the watery gutter,
And an old visage
Smiles back
Wheezing in the mist.
Above and beyond the chorus roars,
But not here.
Stillness crumbles time away;
Alone.
An independent presence is
Contented in its anonymity.
Faded kingdom wrapped in damp.
So clip your cap and cast your glance,
Leave this hollow place.
A memory of a life moved on
A sculpture to a time long gone.

Alison Perry, Cleeve Prior, Worcestershire

MY LOVE STANDS SLENDER AS A REED

My love stands slender as a reed
He knows me not, my heart doth bleed.
His chestnut hair flows long and free
Hazel the eyes that see not me.

Acorns were stolen for skin's glow.
Strength from oak his limbs bestow.
Yet gentle, he treats all the same,
Same soft to lamb as widowed dame.

And when he sings the birds cease flight,
In awe fall silent as if night
Oh could those lips with my lips meet,
And crush between wild strawberries sweet.

Perchance to lie when Phoebus flees,
On camomile neath murmuring trees.
Safe in the arms of my one true love,
And hear him whisper, *Dove, my dove.*

So loud my heart shouts, *love,* so clear,
Would think the stars in heaven could hear.
He hears me not, knows not my need.
My love stands slender as a reed.

Jean M Hill, Stoke-on-Trent, Staffordshire

THE LOST AND FOUND

We are the lost and found,
Sitting hopelessly like dolls in market stalls,
False smiles bruised into cheeks,
Bright eyes ached into faces,
Please pick me, we say, please pick me.
We do not soar through life like paper bags
In summer breezes.
We sit on shelves,
Waiting, impartial to our pain,
Tapping against the mahogony,
And humming lullabies to ourselves.

Chloe Bridget Trumper, Newport, Shropshire

VEGETABLE PATCH

My turn to save the planet
I decide to propagate, rotivate and cultivate
For the very first time, it's a big decision
My other half says my enthusiasm won't last
I dig my plot, add soft, moist compost, home made,
And manure, well rotted
Then I wait for the warm spring days
Which never seem to come
In desperation, my runner beans window high
I plant out my children,
Tethered to ten foot poles into a cold, unforgiving world
Two are eaten almost immediately, my organic dreams
Abandoned and now slug pellets form a neat blue line
Between the ordered rows.
The scorching sun finally arrives and the leaves
Begin to shrivel: is this the end of my dream?

Pam Gosling, Redditch, Worcestershire

POINTLESS PRIZES

If you held the world in the palms of your hands
You'd need more.
If you had all the gold, all the wealth on demand
You'd feel poor.

If you knew of no sorrow, surrounded only by allegiance
You'd feel cold.
If you were the most intelligent, most able and immense
You'd feel old.

It is more than possessions and
Face values that you need.
It is more than tight ties and
Secured prizes you seek.

So, whilst you lounge before the fire in your armchair,
Questions passing through your mind, harsh but so fair.
Was it worth it, this wealth? Truly, was it worth it?
For all that was lost, and now couldn't be shared.

Elizabeth Marshall, Wombourne, Staffordshire

THE SEA

Creator God we praise you for
Bold ocean waves that prance and roar
Tumultuous from shore to shore,
Tumbling, foaming evermore.

We ask you for this day to keep
The seamen stormbound in the deep,
With little time to rest or sleep
Amid the turgid waters' leap.

We thank you for both large and small
Of all sea-creatures, short or tall,
The quaint, grotesque, the comical,
Dwelling where waters deepest fall.

We praise you for each coast and bay,
Where spreads the sea's unstinted spray
To wash the shore, and drain away
As children gather there to play.

We thank you too for liberty
To taste the tang of salty sea,
Which by your own divine decree,
Through ebb and flow is full and free.

Dorothy Headland, Shrewsbury, Shropshire

A CARELESS WORD

A careless word tossed into a sea of upturned faces,
Cuts deep into the flesh of a vulnerable child,
Tell her of her beauty instead, allow her spirit to soar,
On the words you give her, build a ladder of self worth,
She is unique, precious, a child of God,
Crown her princess dreams and kissing frogs,
Laugh with her, make daisy chains and roll in the meadow.
See love reflected in her azure eyes.
Shining luminous above rosy cheeks,
That dimple and hide away sweets.
Reside in the arc of her smile,
For there lies love incarnate.

Louise Pell, Goodrich, Herefordshire

TWILIGHT

A twilight sky is never bright,
It casts no shadows on the dale.

The trees in colour yearn for night,
And touch their beaded breath to grassy trails.

In dusky warm the pheasant sits,
He does not seek for home.

And all his strangled tocks and cricks
Are muted, trembling in the gloam.

My song is wicked, twisted deep,
My breath a cloud of smoke,

With flaming eyes I see the heap,
The sodden earth, and all it chokes.

Hollie Lewis, St Weonards, Herefordshire

North West

THE SECRET GARDENS OF OXTON

Treading gaily across cobbled streets,
Anticipating the glorious colours to come,
We joyfully pass
Into a tiny courtyard garden,
Imaginatively themed to reflect
The proud owner's packed life.
With brains already brimming,
We happily move onto the next garden.
A gasp followed by a flash of photographs,
As we gaze in awe and admiration
At a vibrant rhododendron
As tall as the trees and the house it adorns.
Colourful gardens complemented a wonderful day
As another creative vista
Greets our eager eyes.
Under and around narrow pathways,
Admiring the adults' skill and the child's touch
Bringing a smile to one and all.
What a happy and inspiring day
Spent with man and nature in such harmony.

Esther Sterry, Neston, Cheshire

DEATH OF A LADY

Mrs Robinson died today
But we're not quite sure
When she slipped away.
With her hair neatly combed
And dressed with care.
She spent most of her time
Asleep in her chair.
We discovered her
Round about half past three
When Gladys, the helper,
Was serving tea.
She was a quite little woman
With nothing to say
So nobody noticed
She'd passed away.

Jean Riggini, Manchester, Greater Manchester

LOSS

Awake suddenly, listening, hoping
No whistling tonight
Sounds of talk and laughter but
No whistling tonight

It's fading now that hope
Should be used to it by now
this feeling of loss,
This dark

Smell of smoke
What innocence
Shrouded by the dark
Childish love, painful, wounding
Shrouded by the dark

Frances Heyes, St Helens, Merseyside

ALONE

Grief landmines time.
Each hour I lose a limb.
A single sniper trains his sights upon my heart;
Each bullet bears my name.
An unused cup,
A pair of Christmas trousers never worn,
A magazine of loaded memories.

Grief lies in ambush
In an empty fireside chair,
A threadbare phrase that fells me unawares,
The trailer for the rugby on TV,
Chrysanthemums unwatered in their pots,
The nightime ritual with lock and key:
A fusillade of private parting shots.

Grief strings its tripwires
Through the silent house: a hat, a coat,
A dry toothbrush, an unsigned card
He bought but never wrote.
Unarmed, I soldier on,
Each day a battle in a lonely war.

Penny Kimber, Lymm, Cheshire

LOVE POEMS

I would love to write love
But all I know refuses to flow from either lip or nib.
It is only there when I look deep into your blue, owl eyes.
It is only there when you make my heart somersault with
your words.
It is only there when your bare skin interacts with mine.
It is only there when I daydream about the time I wish to
spend with you.

It is closer where I read the love words of genius
And I feel the invisible magnets
In my chest and in the words
Connect
And they are the words that know exactly my feelings
But will never be mine
And mine will never beautifully, flawlessly convey my love.

Lauren Cooper, Burnley, Lancashire

THE LADYBIRD AND THE WILTING ROSE

The whisper of the rose carried on the breeze
What does it all mean, what is it all about?
When I was just a lonely seed
I had dreams of magnificent deeds
I bow low in the soil, my petals now jaded
My early beauty has almost faded
What has happened to me?

A passing ladybird heard the cry
She stopped to ask the dear rose why?
I beg you not to cry today
For tears will wash your petals away
The passing of time, the effects this makes
Age happens to us all there is no escape
You survive to provide nectar to nourish
We fade to allow those who follow to flourish

Lynn Noone, Swinton, Greater Manchester

DEER IN THETFOLD FOREST

Ethereal light
Threads
Pillars of stark brown trees
Through snow.
Transmogrification;

The ears and eyes
Of the light brown fawn
Startle,
Bruised by car lights and engines,

Ghost talisman
Of youth for Christmas now
And long ago.

Will Ekbery, Wallasey, Merseyside

BEFORE THE RAIN

The clouds press on across the sky
And take no note of you or I.
What heavenly secrets do they keep?
Do they settle, do they sleep?
The answer is they do not stay,
But, ever-changing, make their way
Across the deserts and the seas
With only the winds to try to please.
Sometimes pure as the driven snow,
Sometimes darkly on they go
Ethereal, transient, beckoning,
Here to pause and there to fling
Their diamonds over all the land
From mountain top to desert sand.

Sylvia Wilkinson, Bury, Lancashire

JUST ONE MORE

Just one more, just one more, the plaintive, the plea.
Just one more story, for you and for me.
Not more time for Charlie, for daddy, dogs or work.
Just one little story: when you fell and got hurt?
Or bong up a mountain, her clowning around,
Her boot being swallowed by black boggy ground.
What about Ghandi lifting us all?
Or when you climbed up a hill to the big waterfall?
Tell the story of an Easter, the best one you had,
When Bess ate the chocolate and Bong got all sad.
That Christmas at Nana's all magical, all cold,
When foxy arrived, oh he must be old.
There must be some more, oh, think mummy, think
And I do, as this time could be gone in a blink.
My wide-eyed and thoughtful, my precious delight,
I feel so complete, my heart high as a kite.

Rachel Cole, Astley Village, Lancashire

THINKER

Within a room, within himself
Leasing private thoughts
To pensive hands and thinking features,
Staring to the ground in tempered craze
For the stop he does not want or need
To his perpetual deliberation
And mock absent whole.

The familiar stranger, distinctive unkempt,
Visible and remote to others,
Ideas fermenting behind
The bearded, zipped and buttoned up,
His genteel poverty and inconspicuous passion
Understanding a multitude of voiceless thoughts
Bred and then rehearsed and then repeated
To the workings of an automatic body
And metronome of daily steps.

All that it is to us a silent something,
To him is unceasing symphony.

Lucy Perry, Lancaster, Lancashire

A VOICE IN THE NIGHT

I heard a voice call in the wakeful night,
A voice I thought I knew cried out, as I was on the lip of
sleep.
Was it you?
Or had I misinterpreted a dream of mad desire,
And in the dim glow of that dying fire, heard it -
A pain-wracked sighing from a broken lyre?

Then peace, rose-clad and smiling, came,
Inviting me to sweet repose, while she her vigil kept.
And thus, I slept.

Marjory Houlihan, Bolton, Greater Manchester

LOVE DIVINE

Has Eros touched us yet,
on wing with message to bear
that Love is Divine?
For love is steadfast in the face of Strife,
that harsh sister who lurks in the shadows
ready to twist the arrow deep into the mortal flesh.
And the anguish of love
does not drive away its headiness:
instead we unite in force
for all things good
and potency.
And if it should please
the mighty Aphrodite
we shall abide
within her garments of silk,
for all time.

Liz Kavanagh, Liverpool, Merseyside

PICNIC ON A SUNDAY

Chidren playing in a bluebell wood
Hiding places and a widing road
A dandelion head to tell the time
A rope swing and a tree to climb

A plush grassy bank beside a stream
Fluffy cakes, strawberries and cream
Puppies romping in the long grass
Holding hands walk a boy and lass

Buttercups on the skin cast a golden glow
A babbling brook where waters flow
Girls with daisy chains in the meadow play
A pretty picture painted on a sunny day

Sky of blue above a field of green
Creating such an idyllic scene
Homeward bound under a darkening sky
For Sunday tea and mum's apple pie

June Brooks, Upholland, Lancashire

STILL MISSING

I open once more the door to your room,
bed made-up and unused, still empty,
linger by your wardrobe wondering what
you are wearing today, why and where.

I cross the swollen stream on the stepping stones,
take off shoes and socks, without you.
I pull weeds from the patio whilst the raised beds whisper,
Where is she planting, cutting, tending?

I glance out towards the uncertain shore,
then turn from its comfortless ebb and flow,
I get by on busyness, books and breakfasts,
bolster my now to the crash and roar

Of the waves breaking on shingles and shells,
breaking, breaking, breaking, until,
I hear only myself in the silent throng
of spaces and stillness, where you belong.

John Harrison, Hutton, Lancashire

I AM

I am,
The very first sunrise on the very first day
The light rain tickling perfect skill
The laughter shared with people loved
The rush of warmth felt within

I am,
The virgin footprint in the pure crisp snow
The kiss of a deep embrace
The sudden pop of sparkling champagne
The girl with the perfect face

I am,
The north star shining on a stormy sea
The secrets only dreamers know
The longing for the dark of night
The place I alone can go

Jean Watson, Crosby, Merseyside

UNTITLED

Leaving alone at dawn
passed the party debris.
Slipping out onto the street,
directionless.

Then suddenly over a rise, stretches the silent city.
Domes and towers built on mist
and an engorged sun, pulsing on the horizon.

And in all of the morning, not a sign of life,
But for a trapped bird
Lunging in my breast.

John Reynolds, Prenton, Merseyside

FEBRUARY

The black night climbs,
like unto a mountain range
forming in the ice blue
February skies.
In the stillness
and the rising mist
captured birdsong
echoes across the valley
of solitary, spiky trees.
They clutch the valley slopes,
their bare, twisted branches
reaching forever toward
the fading light of a
winter sunset as the fiery
ball slips slowly into the
grey mist of night.

Muriel Miller, Blackburn, Lancashire

ECLIPSE

I exsist in my small world, waiting.
He exists in his much more complex world, absorbing life.
I am in his orbit.
Like planets drawn by a gravitational pull,
He draws me in and repels me at seasonal intervals.
When his world turns to face mine I'm bewitched,
His presence eclipses my existence.
He turns away, the coldness of winter returns even on
Midsummer.
The disdain, the rejection.
We exist in our own worlds, spinning endlessly,
Until the next time we face each other, smile,
And feel the warmth return.
He sees something, something he wants but doesn't want
to keep.
At least not yet, not this time.
Maybe at the next eclipse.

Elizabeth Ware, Penrith, Cumbria

CAPTAIN ALFRED MAURICE TOYE, MC VC, 1898-1955

I study the face and wonder who he was
I recognise the body
short arms, rounded head, broad chest.
The body of my family. But I do not know the man.
At 19 I was reading Plato in Holborn
He rallied his men from retreat to hold an impossible line
and turn a German advance.
At 20 he fought his way, twice wounded,
through smoke and blood
to regain lost trenches and secure a flank.
I was buying the girl next door a cappuccino
I suspect that when he died, husband and father
A quiet middle class, middle-aged Devon death,
The casing of his shell-splintered soul
Was rusting in French mud.
He looks as though he was tidy
Folding a neat newspaper, putting away polished shoes,
I see only an erect, uniformed stranger
An officer with disdainful eyes
My father's face under the stern peaked cap,
Medals glinting with contempt.

Dennis Toye, Darlton-in-Furness, Cumbria

THE SEA

Such an embodiment of fumbling foam
Requires a lather of sand and shell
Netted together for the rolling waves

Sifting out through time's corrosive calender
The particles become essence we carbon date
Then add to the growth of the world

Heart shapes in the white of a breaker compete
For the likeness rights hanging on the wall
Making motion stand still this last and only moment

Darren Kelly, Southport, Lancashire

A LITTLE RECIPROCATION?

An ocean of unwavering principals. Red, blue, green,
Gently composes an argument, an eye-popping scene.
Behold a preacher! The ultimate streamlined raconteur,
Demanding of attention simply because he is there,
And then, feigning magnanimity, his head turns skywards,
Pulling at will on all manners of moments and witticisms.

Picking coagulated lumps from this information broth,
Yet relentlessly obsequious, raising barely a cough,
He lets a stream of technicolour knowledge pepper his brow
And all we do is seek to extend his visit, delay his final
bow.
So, with a man so well-versed, a conduit to me, to all,
Is a little reciprocation too much to ask from him
Or is society's glorious leader just another brick wall?

Matthew Birchall, Ashton-in-Makerfield, Greater Manchester

PEACE GARDEN

You run, I chase.
rushing and pushing
through the arches of youthful budding green
the sun, dancing through twisting, twining ivy vines and
leafy shoots above,
carves dark mottled shadow blots upon the ground below,
scene from our secret play.
Only You and I understand.
I stop; need swelling as I watch You flee, your footsteps
clamourous, desperate,
pounding against the scattering pebble path.
I breathe vice, eager and alive as I go in for the kill.
I always ran faster, tearing tortuous around the snaking
path.
Your head whips back, eyes earthquakes as they meet
mine.
I am closing in.

Got You. But I never get enough.
You meet me as your maker, pleading sweet mercy.
You know You are a fool.
I sense it. Thirsting for any and every morsel of ground
yielded,
And you. Quenchlessly You.
You run.
I'll always follow.

Rachael Knott, Congleton, Cheshire

IN THE FLOW OF CALM

The air of this day is so easy to breathe.
Calmness has found me with a gentle breeze.
I sit in its hand as it cushions my soul.
In the flow of calm and emotion control.

The summer sun has made all things well.
I could sleep serenely under its spell.
I am almost dazed by how good I feel.
In the flow of calm on life's big wheel.

Today could hand me anything.
I'd peacefully smile and the birds would still sing.
I love days like today when I feel like this.
In the flow of calm and the feeling of bliss.

Yes, I will sleep well this night.
To dream of heaven and eternal life.
It feels like I am holding the hand of life's arm.
May I stay this way, in the flow of calm.

Lee Hughes, Ellesmere Port, Cheshire

TWIST, TURN, SPIN, SPIRAL AND FOLD

Autumn leaves falling
Unprotected old, bare, stark, bleak
Tarnished tatty rags, rent and torn
Undressed, uncovered windswept trees exposed
Meandering, wind snaking through
Naked branches in a stilted wood, coppice, forest grove
Looking ashen, dowdy and arid
Eclipsed by the hue of beaded floor
Autumn leaves falling
Vivid
Ever-changing wonderful colourful array
Stooped low against the sunlight horizon
Feelings caressed by the symphony
Autumn leaves falling
Lifeless
Lament to the soft crackle, crush and crumble of decay
Indigo sky heralds the harvest
Now to gather in and reap the blades
Gold, red, brown, yellow, from green.

Margaret Harris, Chester, Cheshire

North East

PRECIOUS

A turquoise pebble
washed up on a desolate shore;
something different caught my
eye among the taupe and grey.
Its translucent, glowing heart
resonating with mine.

Sea water swirls around
and reveal it's just a nugget
of shingle-worn glass.

But I treasure it all the same.

Fenella Berry, Halifax, West Yorkshire

LIKE A LITTLE MONKEY MAN

A coat of golden down,
such a curiosity,
protective garment of the womb
still worn,
because you came so soon.
Shimmering swirls,
soft as the nap of a rose petal,
delicate as breath.
With silken twists
for each elbow and ear.
A sable hood,
like warm kitten fuzz,
light as air, tickles
my lips and skin as we nuzzle in.
Adorable, dressed in fluff,
my funny little newborn thing.

Sandra Wiggins, Leeds, West Yorkshire

DRIFTING

Night falls
I lose you
Just footprints
In the virgin snow

Stumbling
I call you
Silence lies
Heavily in leaden air

Hope gone
I mourn you
Tears fall
From blinded eyes

Day breaks
I see you
Red and black
Against swirling white

The pinnacle appears
And you hold out your hand

Mary Loy, Bradford, West Yorkshire

GOD'S OWN COUNTY

Yorkshire formed your first perceptions,
framed you, shaped you; what you were
in your youth; your mind's reception
of all you felt and saw and heard.
Sunlit Pennines, millstone grit, grey-veiled
in mist, moors masked in sleet.
Shrouding snowstorms' clothing green strays;
scudding clouds cloak ling and peat.
Yorkshire Dales' white limestone outcrop
dazzling bright in sun and shower;
scrambling scree, rise high, then deep drop
to the beck where grayling glower.
Lowering skies scowl darkly haunting,
wuthering winds prowl, vaunting power;
scarlet sunsets, crimson, flaunting
memories of glorious hours.
All forgotten? Lost in time? So
dimly lit, as memory fades.
Yet you knew this land; as we know;
When those memories first were made.

Margaret Squire, Elland, West Yorkshire

LETTER

I do not say the sending of the letter
Did not cause our friends at work unease:
Here was an affair to make them consider
The hidden-away parts in the life we lead.
They had to rethink us as strangers,
Characters in a book
Who step off the page and amaze us
With a subtle action or shooting of a look.
How we can ever really truly know each other
Is the question they were then lead to ask;
Are we alone even with a lover,
And is it impossible to see into the dark
When the best to be hoped for is empathy,
That mental bridge across the unknown sea.

Patrick Mennell, Hull, East Yorkshire

MY LOVE

My love, my spirit's
temple, you are my
Mecca, my Wailing Wall
my Nirvana, my
bountiful Karma, my
spirit's armour, my heart's
desire, my passion's fire.

My high as a kite, my
love at first sight, my
eternal kiss, my absolute
bliss, my ideal date, my
soulful mate, my infinite
fling, my everything,
my love; that's who you are.

Clare Lupino, Hebden Bridge, West Yorkshire

GOODNIGHT

Say goodnight my dearest
But in some fairer land bid me good morning
Lie your dear body down to rest
Here we lay hand in hand
I fear the lonely day that's dawning

The light from your eyes has gone
You lifeless body so still, so cold
On your dear lips a kiss I plant
The songbirds sing a lonely song
Roses and lilies their petals unfold
The wind a mournful tune doth chant

Think of me beloved when you are gone
To that fairer place
Remember all the happiness we had
For those departed days I long
Empty days, lonely nights, feelings I cannot erase

So say goodnight my darling
Not a final goodbye
But in a fairer place
Bid me good morning

Anna Lawson, Baildon, West Yorkshire

VALLE DE LA LUNA (CHILE)

What hand wrought you?
An exquisite palette
Of shimmering sunsets,
And eerie incandescence.

What voice silenced you?
Layer upon layer
Of undulating stillness
As blood spills, and secrets never told.

What eye stained you?
Melting indigo into gold.
Luminescent green
Leeching into red.

What deity conceived you?
Eternal wishes
Of unity with the other,
Our shield against the elements.

All who are lost now come to search
In your mirage of solitude.
Our ancient selves crying out
To connect in your infinity.

Audrey McIlvain, Scarborough, North Yorkshire

THE VAN

It has stood on the lane for years
Decrepit, but still in one piece
Its sides heavily creased
A back window covered by a board
Weeds engulf the wheels
A scrap fridge leans on a door
Yet it contains so many stories
Journeys, happenings, destinations
Traumas, joy and sadness
Now left forlorn and forgotten
One day men will come
And not even think about its life
But return it to mother earth

Robert Morley, Doncaster, South Yorkshire

THE OLD ROAD

Loose gravel and potholes like the surface of the moon,
Giant sycamores on the left,
Cattle mown fields to the right.
Six cottages at the top of this tractor-worn road,
Uninhabitable in winter paradise in summer,
hazel and elderberry escape through the fence.
Every stride, every step crunching gravel under toe,
Brings back memories of home.
Tattooed in your mind this place is the countryside
This road has worn many a boot or shoe,
Ramblers and city folk sharing this gravel,
On a Sunday afternoon.
Twice a day as schoolboy,
Walking this road I would enjoy.

In daylight or darkest of night I will travel this road,
Until the end of time.

Jerry Dowson, Houghton-le-Spring, Tyne and Wear

157

TRAVELLERS' TALES

Dirty Yorkshire Metro bus with diesel engine
Butting through the traffic jam at half past eight,
With passengers from Garforth, Colton, Crossgates,
To the city centre, they must not be late.

As they go off to the factory, the library, the market,
Plan to buy their groceries in their favourite shop,
They watch the well-known landmarks slipping quickly by
them,
Reach out for the bell and off at their bus stop.

There are customers for Debenhams and Marks and
Spencer.
And girls who work behind the automatic tills.
There are typists, cleaners, porters, jewellers
And waitresses to wipe up all the coffee spills.

There are fresh, young executives in pale grey pinstripes
And builders' apprentices in worn Levis,
Beside the eager office juniors with very strange hairstyles
And trainee accountants wearing paisley ties.

They are all so very busy looking out of the window
Gazing at the morning with a sleepy eye
That they cannot see the other people sitting by them,
They can only count the minutes as their lives slip by.

Lynn Widdows, Harrogate, North Yorkshire

TRAVELLER

I am a traveller, traversing this once great land,
and harken to my masters' whims,
dispatched to where they see fit.
I am forgotten in my own residence, a shadow on the wall.
My name seldom said or heard in
the freehouses of my home.
Except in malice.

I traverse rail and road of this broken isle,
and endlessly trek from one place to another.
never in a single spot for too long,
just another body in a crowd.
My face never remembered in any of the meeting places.
Except that it fades.

I traverse beaten paths of this confused state,
a place opposed to, yet inexorably drawn towards change.
Worn away by the ocean breeze,
yet remain exactly the same.
My likeness, eroded away by the sands of time.
Except that it reanimates.

A time yet to come, to return to my masters,
I shall travel one last time
beyond the stars.

Duane Boyd, Ripon, North Yorkshire

LOVE

An open heart,
Is where all good starts.
Love is everywhere.
It is initiated in silent prayer.
Ssh, be still.
Listen.
A meditation so deep
That through the cracks of brokenness, love does creep.
Intentions that are pure
Are the gateway to be sure.
Believe.
Be open to receive
Love from the heart.

Angela Dinan, Driffield, East Yorkshire

FACING FACTS

The kitchen was a common place
for us to talk, face to face.
The answer I needed might have been
in the peaking folds of cream
Mum was whisking a trifle for tea,
she didn't look directly at me
but hesitated over the question,
I hung on with determination
it seemed to cause her some consternation.
She paused at great length for inspiration
ironic that even after six children
the facts of life could still be troublesome.

The hardest fact of life came later
as loss and gain learned to breathe together.

Anne Broadbent, Holmfirth, West Yorkshire

CUCKOOS

A dozen cuckoos in my brain
Have built their twisted nest
At three a.m. their shrill refrain
Eviscerates my rest.

They twitter, flitter ceaselessly,
Their wings disturb my thought
A feathery cacophony
In throbbing temples wrought.

Enough, desist, your end is nigh
I warn my squawking flock.
I'll bake you in a cuckoo pie
Or stuff you in a clock.

What incantation can I speak
To end this pre-dawn chorus?
Your arcane name? A wizard's shriek:
Cuculus canorus.

Still here? A truce, my wingèd foes,
My avian affliction.
Roost in peace now, let me doze,
Or else confront eviction.

Gavin Extence, Sheffield, South Yorkshire

THE AGE OF INNOCENCE

We are cuckold by our nature, drowned in fancy clothes
We wear; do not sit and beg its reason, less
The threads begin to tear. So primitive life can seem
To charge the bud before it falls; to stop the dreams
And curse the flowers, a severed break, not clean.

Who is innocent? What's to gain? When man is cornered
In a frame sucked in a whirlpool of desire, the
Trap is set, it has the power to chard the embers of
A fire: dawn has many regions bridging life to life
Seeking penetration, rallying to be loved.

Sometimes the wind even sighs, when air fans
The sleeping breeze, boughs break to say goodbye,
Fruit tempting in its dark disguise
To be estranged from
The tree of life.

Optimism, poems bleat the springtime noon;
Lambs innocent in their stare,
Untainted nature fresh with dew, the
Grass is green, it doesn't care,
I drink the fruit that's not impaired.

Philip Cranswick, Rotherham, South Yorkshire

THE FAN

Behind the velvet drapes she trembles
The hansom cab that smelt of new leather is gone.
Once, and only once did he smile
But now the gin is all that resembles
Her chamfered time.
The flowered oak boards of foot-worn lime
And the bent cane chair she sits upon
Are cold, a tuba plays a ragtime tune
Vänta, vem är det? Nej, know
You will be gone in a day or so
Below a fan of silken lace they stare at your body
But not your face
Like looking at a sky without a moon

Derek Greenacre, Morpeth, Northumberland

ROUGH SEA

Today, due to yesterday's storms,
The Mediterranean is a cross and angry sea.
Relentlessly waves crashing noisily into the shore line.
Earlier, out to sea, the white horses rode the waves.
We sat on a sheltered bench catching the last of the sun,
Watching and listening to the power of the sea.
Hearing the rattling sound of pebbles
Picked up and dropped again.
Later, when the sky turned black, the pale sun hid itself.
Drama appeared in the wind driven clouds across the sky.
No seabirds to see now, they've moved inland to the lake.
Well wrapped-up people, walking quickly into the wind,
Rushing back to warm hotels and apartments
Before the rain comes.

Marjorie Lacy, South Elmsall, West Yorkshire

KNOWING

Our problem-solving science
Science can fix it
The ways of our world
Science explains it
The stars and beyond
Science can see it
Our spiritual ideals
Science avoids it
So, what of God?
Religion embraces it
With so many creeds
Religion never mixes it
When we are ill
Medical mends it
Till we are too ill
Then medical's lost it

There is an ancient knowing
A growing faith in who we are
Older than science, religion and medicine
And more effective for our living, by far

David Thomson, Newcastle-upon-Tyne, Tyne and Wear

WINTER MOON OVER HADRIAN'S WALL

On the far flung hillside
A mile over the valley
And towards the
Badlands of the north
The winter moon is racing
And with it comes the snow

Beyond Crag Lough,
The ghostly silence
Of a winter night
Seems to give way
To the tramp of hobnails,
And the guttural shouts of men

Just as quickly silence returns
And on this cold December night
A hush descends
Over the frozen wilderness
Of the Roman Empire

Rob Turnbull, Haltwhistle, Northumberland

HAPPINESS

An evasive force we sometimes feel
To skim our thoughts
Arrest our dreams
Can money buy it? Seems not
Lest millionaires would
Have the lot
Yet it's all around us
If we open our eyes
From feeling good to every smile
The pleasure of love
Received and given
The wonder found
In all that's living

Kathleen J Jinks, Middlesbrough, Cleveland

THE ANTS

"Just look at all those ants,"
God said one sunny day.
"See that pompous fat one,"
God smiled in his godly way.
"Look how he bullies all the others,
As they run from tree to tree,
He thinks he's so important,
He's forgotten about Me.
Yes, and look at all the workers
Busy as can be,
It seems they haven't time now,
To remember about me.
They've really got their jobs to do,
So important, yes I see
Oh dear, my eyes are failing:
Celestial glasses, Gabriel, please.
These aren't ants!" ...

Elaine D Scullion, Dunston, Tyne and Wear

PARADISE REGAINED

It's when swallows return.
It's when the beech is coppered.
It's when the earth is lush with green.
It's when water chants over stones.
It's when the skylark sings.
Bliss distilled.
Stored in the soul.

It's the fragrance of the rugosa rose
It's the blue of cornflower.
It's the wonder in a child's eye.

It's the melt of chocolate,
It's the touch of the sun,
It's the essence of snow,
It's the trance of stars.
Bliss distilled,
Stored in the soul.

Mary Atkinson, Alnwick, Northumberland

THE COUNTRY LANE

I knew that if I sat there
For long enough, one day
Spring would turn to summer
And green grass into hay.
But, somewhere patience withered,
No longer I remained
Than takes a bee to gather
One golden pollen strain.
Yet now, as old I sit here,
The thoughts of that same day
Are like a dewmoist morning
Heralding a glorious day.
Yes, autumn follows quickly
With winter on its heel
But yet there's time for wonder
As each new day begins.
Life never need be lonely
If each day we relearn
To live and love and laugh
Like that child
In the country lane.

Jennifer Gordon-Russell, Morpeth, Northumberland

SIBERIA REMEMBERED

I walked among the many dead
And shunned the unknown corpses
I watched the guards with frozen smiles
Grind wretched glimpses into files of ice
That glittered with the sorrow
The death head glint of man's tomorrow.

Betty Hewitt, Darlington, County Durham

YESTERDAY

Yesterday
when we walked
hand in hand
down the avenue
of togetherness
and we stopped
at the corner
shop selling love

and
further down the
road was tomorrow
bathed in a white
light with no shadows

and
I turned my heart
to face yours

Jack Howard, Crook, County Durham

IN TANDEM

We escaped at dawn, cycling silently from the village,
the only sound our breathing and the whirr of wheels
in tune with nature,
A dog barking, and birds' chorus,
the smell of early morning,
we were truly alive.
Daylight bled over the fields, hay turning from grey to
pale yellow, as valleys cleared of low hanging mist.
We crested the hill, and there it was,
The sweep of the forest,
A magic doorway where the world ceases to exist,
Corn shining, in a distant field a tractor with circling birds,
Spiders webs shining with dew.
We wobbled as I looked back, a pale patch of sky, receding
dark clouds threatening, as the world disappeared.
In tandem, among nature's secrets,
a rawness with no sense of time or place,
peddling in harmony.
The sky now bitten into by dark branches, everything alive
in this magical place, free-wheeling along the track
to nowhere.

George Carrick, Cramlington, Northumberland

INTO THE LIGHT

Hurled, curled, into this world.
Slung, slipping and sliding, into the light.
With a sense of unknowing,
Where I was going.

Lost, tossed, into a sea of faces.
Glimpses of places, vague and forgotten,
Permeate my being, in blurred separateness.
With a sense of longing, yet not belonging.

Tempered, tested, taunted and tattered
Buffeted and battered. Until nothing mattered.
Forged by a force, where form was reformed.

Transmuted, transcended, this transient traveller
Journeying back home from the land of the homeless.
Liberated, uplifted into a portal of light
Now blissful, illumined, awakened insight.

Irene Anderson, Leadgate, County Durham

Northern
Ireland

SONNET 2

Often I wondered why the changeless stars
That sparkle in the dark unclouded sky
Should waste their beauty on this world of ours
And lend us rays of cosmic sympathy
And, too, I wondered why night's silent queen
Bathed in the glory of the lunar day
Should shed her radiance o'er our thankless scene
Nor turn her proudly tender face away
Then did my mute, delighted eyes behold
Like sunshine on a performed morn in June
The rosebud of your loveliness unfold
And wonder I no more at stars and moon
For your beauty, alike in heart and eyes
Commands the graceful homage of the skies

Hubert Boyle, Magherafelt, Northern Ireland

LEAVING FOR UNIVERSITY

My bags are packed, my passport ready
The letter of acceptance tucked inside.
My father says goodbye, in a voice not quite steady
September sun glows, I shan't be back till snow.

If I appear fine, then I am faking
Like the squirrel we once almost ran over
Fright acted like poison. It started shaking
And faced with our car the giant, it froze.

But just as ice must melt and leaves must fall
I must leave to make my change in me
Just as bluish dawn must hear sun's call
I must leave to start new things.

Niamh O'Kane, Limavady, Northern Ireland

THE TREE

The tree stood out
That night,
So wise and erect,
Luminous fingers splayed
Against a desolate sky,
And I knew then
That each ancient branch
Had once bent
And caressed
A stranger passing by;
An illicit lover;
A despondent *thumber,*
Or perhaps
Someone lost,
Like I,
Who rendered and slept
In the unfurled arms
Of its lichen bed.

Rosie Hogan-Diamond, Ballymena, Northern Ireland

CONFERENCE BLUES

Sat in the dusty conference room
I'm longing to be free
Though wit and humour sparkle here
It's not the place for me

Outside the April sun shines down
The sky is clear and blue
A light breeze stirs the daffodils
Of green and saffron hue

Just now Ambition holds the floor
With arrogance and pride
He seeks by word and turn of phrase
The rest to override

And as he does Dame Nature speaks
In accents soft and low
Oh please declare the motion closed
And leave me free to go!

James Wilson, Ballyclare, Northern Ireland

Wales

LOVE

As bitter as tonic water
Slimline
Prior to gin

Greasy seaweed
Languishing
Over travelled

Damp skin entwined
Condensation
Reeking down

Dull as candle light
Dazzling as faultless clouds

It speaks in unknown tongues
Fluent as a phrase book
Raged as time itself

Dressed in grey
That perpetual stare
Without sight

Unequivocally alone

Amy Angharad Jones, Cowbridge, Wales

SPECIAL DELIVERY

Little card says my name
Heart swells, eyes bulge
For me?

They're in a white vase
Thick, ceramic
With a green bow on its chest

White lilies burst
Like stars of purity
A symbol of femininity
Intoxicating and sweet

I take a moment to absorb it
Paralysed by their beauty
Lost in the gesture

When he sees them, he will be jealous
Confused by the fact a woman gave a gift
That could evoke so much emotion in me
And he'll know what I'm thinking

Who needs men
When you've got great friends?

Karla Brading, Merthyr Tydfil, Wales

ISSUS 333 B C

The lions of ancient stone stare through
The passing of two thousand years
Greek and Persian here once knew
The heat, the dust, the pain, the tears

Beyond the Payas river's northern bound
The winged lion empire flaunted power
Where upstart Macedonian claimed the ground
And fevered armies faced each other's ire

The phalanx drives and mighty Ashur reels
Blinded with sweat and blinded by sun
Persians fall beneath their sagging shields
Are crushed by screaming chariot wheels
And the brave, unyielding, overrun

The lions of ancient stone still stare
Blind to the passing of two thousand years
No stones record, no monuments declare
The deeds of heroism suffered there
In heat, in dust, in pain, in tears

David Cirell, Glamorgan, Wales

ODE TO A HGV DRIVER

Up at the crack
Out of the sack
Safely securing his load
Bacon and bread
Sauce that is red
Café at the end of the road

Fags on the dash
Crumbs in moustache
Forty four tonnes on his back
Towns trundle by
Leicester, Corby and Rye
A yawn, a cough and a hack

A lay by for a kip
The long lonely trip
Variable speed limit camera
Traffic jam queues
Motorway blues
The life of a heavy goods driver

Simon Hicks, Chepstow, Wales

SPOKEN IN HASTE

If only we could reclaim words
Untongue them from the unforgiving air
Where lingering unleashed, they lacerate
A target hit, a point scored
Opponent crushed, friend turned to foe
Venom inflicted in a tongue's flick
Or worse, the unintentional barb
Piercing the hearts of those held dear

If only words could be reclaimed
Replaced with what we should have said

Janet Williams, Newport, Wales

CLEAR STREAM

My mind has been a clear stream flowing
In the winter it has been sparkling icy, piercing to touch
and hard
But in the summer it changes into a fragrant balm of
sensual pleasure unparalled
When I dip my body naked in to its curling waters
In the spring it strokes my stiff limbs like a healing hand
Softening, melting the ache of effortful days
And in the autumn the dying summer sky lays its colours
down
Into playful reflection, shimmering still with a youthfulness
Lost by all else.
Yes, my mind has been a clear stream flowing
And I dip my pen into its waters
Remembering

Joanne Newton, Cemmaes, Wales

IN THIS LIFE

What in the world do we do in this life
When all around is war and strife?
What in this life for the love of our Lord
When all shall wield the gun and the sword?
What in this life is still good and true
When he hates me and I hate you?
How in the world will our planet survive
When no animals or trees are left alive?
Who in this life do the hungry ask
When famine and death wear a daily mask?
What in this life are our neighbours here for
When the opposite house slams fast its front door?
Here in this life should the lessons be learned
The world is our brother, kinship not spurned
Here in this life is but the one choice
To cry out the truth with humanity's voice
Here in this life, made unique as we are
Our blue, beautiful world, our home, our star

Jean Ruston, Talybunt-On-Usk, Wales

NIGHT THOUGHTS

What became of the girl that was me?
Long days in the sun
On the sand
By the sea
Dreaming of love

Winter nights by the fire
With friends of my heart
Talking of love

Salt spray in my face
As I walked the coast path
With the love of my life

Where now is the girl that was me
Lover, wife, mother, now widow
But still
In my mind
The girl that was me

Vera Phillips, Newport, Wales

MOUNTAINS OF THE MIND

The mountains are calling to me.
Their power pulls me back, reels me in.
Like a moth to a flame I am drawn to the place where my
spirit is free.
Where I feel nature's warmth upon my face, her breath
upon my skin.
There I can be alone and at one with the universe.

But what is this magic that calls to me?
Is it their majesty or timeless beauty?
Could it be the history that surrounds them?
Or is it the memory of places I walked when I was young?
Maybe it's all of them, or maybe it's none of them.

For although I no longer live among them, they still live
within me.
And if I cannot walk on their sunkissed slopes
Or smell the grass on an evening breeze,
I shall steal away from the tedium of the day and
Walk on mountains of the mind and hillsides of
imagination.

Lindsay Hurlow, Swansea, Wales

WAY OF LIFE - MODUS VITAE

My yesterdays are before you
Two thousand Sundays today.
Our times tick slowly towards
Their start and letters wait
Words and pen,
Reliving each second of years apart.

Those far-off futures beyond the dark
Those slow-turning ways that dream you there.
It seemed that ever waiting was slipping away
And fading to days of before
And of where.
How life has patterned the reasons to stay.

Your words remain outside of me
Though your dreams are ages old.
The breath of day and last word breaking
The chords of truth and the first light meaning
There is no prospect to life without dreaming.

Peter Hughes, Anglesey, Wales

SEARCH

I went looking for the past
Long shafts of sunlight
Left the road for darkness
Fog crept in ruthlessly
And the thorn trees
Forked more than usual
Leaning dangerously
In the growing night

Did you find
What you were searching for?
No, I only found
Memories of seasides full of joy
Days with no fear
Endless days without time

Only an hourglass was left
Empty and old
Rusting with the tides

Janet Hughes, Montgomery, Wales

DIOMEDES

Beneath the hoary ripened sash
A drunken belching calabash
A swooping troop of swallow tails
Fall to fill the ragged gash

Step out a fettered ingenue
Her limbs of milk and honey hue
She bends her back to nought but fails
To halt the tide she's born to rue

Along the serried ranks of strata
Angels weep a mute cantata
A kiss to fan a thousand sails
In deathless hope inamorata

Richard Lloyd, Newcastle Emlyn, Wales

VERSIFICATION

Great mage, your timeless words have ravished me
Sent from the glowing hearths of lost tradition
Withal that mythic face we'll never see
Are echoes heard of your sweet manumission

Though scarce could you have known how was your quill
To cast the inky tendrils of your might
Along time's tunnel where still breathing, still
It passes in to future's blinding sight

Infinite generations yet to be
Will wonder at your convoluted art
Why then you played the game to set them free?
Enjoining them in one place, at the heart

There fondly in that chamber to remain
Eternally to echo your refrain

James Hayward, Bargoed, Wales

HIS LOVE

He is the gentle breeze
After the storm
Of everything
That was wrong with your life
Before him.
He somehow whispered by
Touched your soul and
Chased away
The evils of your past.
With the simplicity of a
Warm smile and secure arms
He erased all your fears and worries
Turned your life around and
Gave you what you always dreamt of.
Maybe he'll never realise it
Or perhaps he already does
But his love is what your life is about.

Lianne Jones, Cardiff, Wales

Scotland

DANTE TO VIRGIL AT THE GATES OF PARADISE

Goodbye my friend
For you a journey's end and
Me the point where love is found
To start renewed in paradise
Upon the holy ground

Tears are falling with my love
For comradeship and leadership you did love
Free will of kindred spirit
Keep me strong in times of need
On the way though long

Farewell the guide and friend beside
The gates of Eden now stand wide
You who showed me faults of man
Each passion that was material, damn
Bid one question, shades below
Each answer for myself
That I must know

Matilda comes now to wash me so
As you depart through my tears
I watch you go
Farewell, friend

N J Bain, Duns, Scotland

THE LAST POST

I last saw my country
When it was already
Older than the rocks
That kept the sea
Teathered
Older than the sea
That bleeds the rocks dry
And is kissed awake
By the sun with
The lure of a lover's joy
That lilts through every vein
In company with every
Footprint that passed
Over every terrain
I last saw my country
And it last saw me
Fast disappearing
Bloodstained
For its tapestry

Gabriel Dennis, Blairgowrie, Scotland

A GLASGOW ROMANCE

A drunk man
Buying eight bottles of beer
With ninety pence of coppers
Foraged from roadside gutters
Kissing the cashier's hand
He, an ancient knight
Accepting a sacred quest
And she, the Lady Opiate
Bequeathing a lifetime's purpose
To those January fingers
It is a Glasgow romance
An almost perfect, almost love song

Julie Martis, Hamilton, Scotland

ON A VISIT TO WESTMINSTER ABBEY

Beneath my feet great statesmen lie
With poets, princes, men of dye
Whose deeds in generations past
Declared them of immortal cast.

And even now, though tightly cased
And robbed of sense and sight and taste,
These noble spirits, born to strife,
Persist in tantalising life.

But even mighty stone wears thin
Beneath the scuffling weight of sin
And all too soon, though bright as hay
Those golden letters fade away.

Thomas Craig, Hamilton, Scotland

MAGDALENE BLACK

Magdalene Black hair slicked back to a fine
Chinois knot. Immaculate Magdalene Black sat
on the end of our row in the fourth form class, smugly

Magdalene Black. Unliked for the most part
she'd spent her days buying friends with like me vouchers
from itunes and Debenhams. Trade our fake fur

coats for her real thing, try to convince us
Each bag was spare and she really didn't like it. It was a
gift
And we'd take it, slag her off behind her back

see if we could make her cry. We'd try, leave her sitting
on her own, she never needed to share. We wouldn't let her
Magdalene Black, mother too posh to bear a Mary

J Elliott, Ayr, Scotland

STAR DANCING

I contemplate a flawless sky
Fractured by winter branches
Reflectively I wonder why
The stars enact their dances

Inscrutably they twinkle down
As they wander timeless paths
Like jewels upon a velvet gown
The hands of gods have cast

From their complex patterns shine
Ancient wisdom of the past
Rich knowledge of a different time
Holds secrets, deep and vast

Are answers there for us to see
Or are they deep inside
The answers that would set us free
Within where gods reside

I contemplate an endless sky
For my questions I seek answers
In my dreams my soul can fly
And the stars and I are dancers

Carole Bone, Glasgow, Scotland

STREAM AT THE MILL

A seamless stream
Flooding with deep memories
Of mills and machines
Unceasing

Clattering contraptions
Deafened and drowned
Bent beings who laboured
Within its whirlpool

Now a shawl of water
Spreads over smooth shiny stones
Like liquid lace

Patricia Turner, Dalbeattie, Scotland

THE EQUINOX

What a battle
The ice maiden
Shows her strength still.
Snow lying thick on the ground
And the dazzling yellow and purple
Of the crocuses peeping through.
Five days to equinox
The green, the growth
The earth mother
Reclaims the frozen ground.
She is reawakening after
Her slumbers
The snow, the earth, the sun
The air is raw with change.

Josephine Sumner, Tain, Scotland

EMBROIDERY

Auntie always had a needle in her hand
and as she sat flat-footed at her stand
laying stitch on stitch, her sewing formed
it's own momentum, in, out, in, out, lawn,
once white, flashing glorious reds and greens
soft hued by pastels woven in between

Her knacky fingers harnessed the exactness
of tricky stitches that she first practiced
as a child. Soundly told the devil made work
for idle hands, and obedient to the kirk
she sewed sweet angels, saints in fields of corn
but peeking through the stalks, the devils horns

She wasn't a fuddy duddy aunt, not one bit
but feisty, full of laughter and a quirky wit
that made us gasp at auntie's naughtiness
fearing someone else might hear, but loving it.
She died too young. But now I see her craft,
her unbowed spirit, and through my tears, I laugh

Muriel Ferrier, Dundee, Scotland

CAROUSEL

While old men remember the steps of life's dance
And young men rejoice in the waltz of romance
While blossoms soar high on warm summer wings
And fall back to earth as the cold winter stings

While shores meet the seas and dissolve into one
And earth ploughs its course ever nearer the sun
While life shines its light on a babe newly born
And death casts the living in darkening mourn

While stars fill the heavens with genesis bright
And God meets religion and ponders its plight
While silent majorities listen in hope
And angels fight demons in cinemascope

Young hearts will delight in love's lingering bliss
While war calls the living to death's final kiss
We puppets will dance to the tune of our master
As life's carousel spins round ever faster

Brian Sutherland, Prestonpans, Scotland

TRIBUTE TO VINCENT

Painting gave him liberty
From indigo pain
Each brush-stroke nearer an imagined heaven
Strewn with stars
A haven of unsurpassed brilliance
Coercing colours
Into immortality
A sorcerer among men
Only when he died
Did they say *hello*

Maggi Macleod, Caithness, Scotland

TO MY LOVER, OVER THE HILLS AND FAR AWAY

An ecstacy of wonder gripped my soul
When I saw you lying on the couch asleep
Like a child so innocent and soft
In beauty so may all the angels keep

I wonder where you journeyed at that time
Your soul was roving on in bliss and peace
Unconscious, lovely, so relaxed, you're mine
One hand lay dropped, in all the grace unknown

I would not wake you ever, still it seems
You were so happy lost in dreams
A moment caught in time was crystallised
Eternity sits always by our side

Teresa Doughty, Fife, Scotland

THE BLACKBIRD'S SONG

I hark back to an evening long ago, when
The song of a blackbird echoed on ripples of sunlit air
Transparent waves, lyrical, the edge of the night wind
Cirrus clouds of insects inert
Dunnocks warbled hidden in rugged branches of hawthorn
The land of my memories, distant and foreign

That summer's eve lingers within the rooms of my mind's
eye
I waited on my friend in the shaded maze of privet hedges
Then, we headed through woodland glades where the song
Of the blackbird was resonant, sweet sounding and
luminous
Like the characters we played, laughter through the trees
Carried transcendent on a broom-scented breeze

Recollections embraced by the song of a lone blackbird
Equivocal vigils, we should have been asleep
The stream glittered with beams of quivering light
From a crescent moon and Venus shining bright

Jacqueline Bain, Paisley, Scotland

THE DANCE OF THE ELECTRONS

The morning light tumbles gracefully
Down her woven path. Coyly
She greets the impassive cliff and
Slips quietly through his grainy sand

Behind the stoic facade
There is a sudden eruption
As she whips the charges into a ragged jig

Their hot ambition jousts and twirls
As they dance, bewitched
Grabbing at her burning heat

But she teases with fickle indulgence
And laughs cruelly, skipping lightly away
Covered modestly in a sheet of cloud

Begging her not to go
They suddenly feel the slump
As their muscles seize up

They whimper back into the cold
Cherishing their bruises in a drugged torpor
Awaiting the next jolt of ecstacy

Valerie MacGregor, Edinburgh, Scotland

FEELINGS

Life is great, life is love
Everything perfect, people smiling
Sky and seas, bright and blue
The world as it should be
Eyes sparkling, always happy
This is me, with you

Darkness in sunshine
Silence amidst laughter
Dread in the brightness
Despair on awakening
Hope gone, heart hurting, void beckoning
This is me, without you

Linda Mackie, Saltcoats, Scotland

IVY

Ivy, companion to time
Loses not its leaves, as others may
Bold, glossy, silent they remain
As one year ends and another begins
The less permanent leave their mark
Each autumn, as with decay
They shed their all, as if
Baring their very souls
Until the leafy cycle begins
Once again, spring sunshine
Filters through, warming the
Chill of their hearts
Yet ivy remains still, silent
Weathering the cold until the sun
Once more reflects on its leaves
Bold, glossy it remains
A companion to time

Jane Ritchie, Dundonald, Scotland

A VEIL OF WEIGHTED MUSLIN

A veil of weighted muslin
Drenches a crimson frame
It ripples in the darkness
Dramatic in its romance

A vale of ash grey
Rolls under a speckled sky
It undulates gently in a scattered breeze
Shifting still through a wrinkled dust

A tower of twisted metal
Points to a thunderous sky
It cuts the storm in a shiver of black
Gothic in its horror!

An ache of silver snow
Stretches through the aisle
Dragging ribbons of folded flesh
To rest

Silent beneath lines of green

Golden under the ever-sinking sun

Laura Bennison, Whitecairns, Scotland

THE PROGRESS VANDALS

They came
Folding the untidy horizon down
So no unruly branch would breach the symmetry
Then they saw the land naked, and ashamed
And they wept for what they had done

Seeking answers
They shouted questions
But no solutions came
Only echoes from the void

With no shadows for the sun to eat
She may starve
And the moon, unable to peek-a-boo with wild things
May give up hope and leave

Then they will stare
And wonder what they might do
With their clean slate
Maybe plant trees

Rona Harvey, Brodie, Scotland

AND SO IT BEGINS

It's cosy, so cosy in here, floating, listening
To the muted sounds, rhythmic, soothing.
I could stay here forever, cocooned in comfort
But wait
Something's wrong
They're clamouring, shouting, urging me to leave
I can't do it, I won't do it
The noises get louder, then
With a *push* and *whoosh*
I'm out into this unfamiliar place,
Strange hands lifting me, scaring me, until
There's a comforting presence in this cold new world
And she's crying and kissing me, holding me close.
And so I meet - my mother

Myra Wimpenny, Kirkcaldy, Scotland

LAST NOTES

Strains of muted music strain the ear
But swell to full when fanfared waves
Are breaking at the flood.

These dangerous sounds, released by friction;
Lip on mouthpiece, fingertip on string
belong to any age

And speak in language, beyond the need of words,
As old as man, and never learned
Until the music stops

Even a world in murderous mode can sing.
Mozart also lived in Auschwitz
And travelled with them as they died.

Chris Cameron, Kelso, Scotland

THE WITCHES' TREE

A tree bewitched and shunned
Standing alone in the grey woods which shrink
Back from its dark magic and recoil from
It's skeletal frame smothered in winter's cold breath
Still and unyielding against the wind's icy blast
Not governed by the rain or gentle sunlight
A force within the grain and sap trying to take shape
A form which eludes the close study of the eye
Branches turn and twist and crisscross their fingers
Unnaturally it bends and stretches arms
That reach down to rake and rend the dark earth
That one looping branch, curling
Upwards and over
A scorpion's tail, poised to strike
And prick with poisonous precision
Come spring, will this skeleton flesh
Out its body in dark green leaf?
Shall it take life and tear
Itself from the earth? The green man
A legend of the forests old

John McGowan, Annan, Scotland

£1,000 to the winner

All top poets never miss sending an annual entry for the National Poetry Anthology. Even if you have won through previously, and had your poetry published in it, this free competition is always open to you. And as it's the only big free poetry competition of its kind, it's the first one you should put on your list to submit your work to. It's the biggest free annual poetry competition in the UK. Around 250 winners are selected every year, each one representing a different UK town. All winners are published in the National Poetry Anthology and all receive a free copy of the book. Many of these poets have never been published before. Send up to THREE poems (on any subject) up to 25 lines and 160 words each (a blank line counts as one line), by the annual closing date of **June 30th** to -
United Press Ltd Admail 3735, London EC1B 1JB
Tel 0844 800 9177
www.unitedpress.co.uk
One overall winner also receives a cheque for £1,000 and the National Poetry Champion Trophy.

Another £1,000 to be won

A poem about someone or something from your home town can win you a top prize in this annual competition. Anyone can submit up to three poems for the competition. The top poem will win £1,000 cash. There is no age limit and no entry fee.

"The poem can be about something or someone from the poet's home area," explained United Press Publications Director, Peter Quinn. "It can be descriptive, historic, romantic, political, or personal - anything you like, as long as there is some local connection.This competition is open to anyone and is completely free to enter - so what have you got to lose?"

Send up to THREE poems, up to 25 lines and 160 words each (a blank line counts as one line), by the annual closing date of **December 31st** to the above address.

NEW BOOK IS A BOOST FOR BARNARDO'S

Don't you wish you'd written down some of the funny things you've heard kids say?

Well someone has - and they've put them all in a book to help raise cash for Barnardo's.

"Things Kids Say" is out now (£5.99) and half of the cover price goes straight to the well-known children's charity. This hilariously funny book was launched by actress and TV celebrity Lynda Bellingham at a Barnardo's centre, and it includes 130 pages of comical real things that have been said by real kids - along with illustrations.

"The book proves that kids are by far the best comedians. All the submissions have been provided by people from all over the UK and all the 13 artists gave their services free," said Peter Quinn, managing director of United Press, which has launched the book.

"To cut out the middle-man and make sure that as much of the revenue as possible goes to Barnardo's, we aren't selling the book in shops. You must order it direct."

For your copy, send £5.99 (plus £1.99 postage & packing) made out to 'United Press' to United Press, Admail 3735, London, EC1B 1JB. £3 from every copy sold goes direct to Barnardo's. Postage is free if you order two or more copies.

To order by credit/debit card phone 0844 800 9177.